living the ZEN arts

living the ZEN arts

MEDITATION • MARTIAL ARTS • CALLIGRAPHY
FLOWER-ARRANGING • THE ART OF TEA

ANDY BAGGOTT

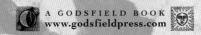

A GODSFIELD BOOK
www.godsfieldpress.com

This book is dedicated to my daughter Lara.

First published in Great Britain in 2005 by Godsfield Press
a division of Octopus Publishing Group Ltd
2–4 Heron Quays, London E14 4JP

Distributed in the United States and Canada by
Sterling Publishing Co., Inc.
387 Park Avenue South, New York, NY 10016-8810

A CIP catalogue record for this book is available from
the British Library

ISBN 1 84181 265 X
EAN 9781841812656

10 9 8 7 6 5 4 3 2 1

Printed and bound in China

CONTENTS

INTRODUCING ZEN

'Just as the great ocean has one taste, the taste of salt, so also this Dharma and Discipline has one taste, the taste of freedom. The gift of Dharma excels all gifts. The taste of Dharma excels all tastes. The delight in Dharma excels all delights.'

BUDDHA

THE FOUNDATIONS OF ZEN

This book presents you with the opportunity to change your life forever; not because its author is a great teacher or writer, but because the subject of this book is one filled with simple but profound wisdom. Zen Buddhism is not just a religion; it is a way of being. Its principles are applicable to any life, anywhere in the world. It teaches mastery of the Self and, through this teaching, shows us all how we can dramatically improve the quality of our lives and bring them into balance and harmony. Modern living is complex, yet shallow. Our lives are often filled with a hectic routine of work and chores giving us little or no time to really enjoy ourselves. Zen wisdom is simple yet deep, and when applied to modern living it can dramatically change our perceptions and deepen our experience of even the most mundane of tasks. Zen is magic and to live a life by following Zen principles is to experience life as an adventure filled with endless discovery and magic. Magic does not mean supernatural, what it means is that Zen teaches about a quality of life in such a way as to make it accessible to anyone and everyone, making its results appear magical.

In this book you will discover something of the history of Zen, its Buddhist origins and its principles. You will also learn how to apply these principles in your everyday life. Zen stories will inspire you on your path of learning and help you understand the seemingly cryptic messages behind some of the Zen philosophy. You will learn how to meditate and through this to make your life a living meditation. You will also find many practical exercises that you can do so that you can experience some of the many benefits of this simple way of living.

The Zen path is a practical way of living life to the full. You can practise it when you arrange a simple vase of flowers, when you drink a cup of tea and even when you wash and dress. You will learn the art of mindfulness, the power of letting go and the ability to turn apparently negative situations into positive outcomes. Above all you will learn to change your mind; to choose a different way to see the world, one that eases suffering and fills you with joy. Have no fear, for according to Zen you cannot make any mistakes, only find lessons to learn.

'Plunge boldly into the Beyond, then be free wherever you are.'

SHOITSU

It is easy to admire the beauty of these Buddhist temples. Zen teaches you to appreciate the beauty of your inner temple.

WHAT IS BUDDHISM?

Before we ask ourselves the question 'What is Zen?' we must first go back in time some one thousand years before Zen came into being. The reason for this is that Zen is a form of Buddhism so in order to understand Zen, one first has to ask the question, 'What is Buddhism?' In around 563 BCE, in what is modern-day Nepal, a boy was born into the noble family of Gautama and the name chosen for him was Siddhartha. Shortly after his birth, his father called upon the local fortune-tellers to divine what the boy's future might hold. He was told that his son was no normal child and that his path would take him one of two ways, either he would succeed his father on the throne and become a world conqueror or he would forsake his heritage and become a world redeemer. Needless to say, his father desired the former of the two paths and did all in his power to steer the boy in the direction of his birthright.

Siddhartha grew up into an exceedingly handsome young man and at the age of 16 married a neighbouring princess called Yasodhara who bore him a son, Rahula. His father, in order to protect his son from the vulgarities of rural life, ordered that whenever Siddhartha left the confines of his palace, that runners went on ahead to clear the streets of any unpleasant sights such as the sick or dying. Apparently the order was not fully carried out because on four occasions, the young man saw 'Four Passing Sights' that changed his perception of the world. First he saw an old man with broken teeth and leaning on a staff, trembling. Next he saw a body wracked with illness lying beside the road. Then he saw a corpse and on the fourth occasion he met a monk who spoke of a path that renounces the world.

These sights so affected the young Siddhartha that at the age of 29 he left his wife, child and noble life to walk a path of learning. He first sought out two Hindu masters and learned much about their tradition and understandings. Next he joined a group of travelling ascetics and sought to master his mind and body through fasting. It is said that he got to a level where he was eating just one grain of rice a day and that he became so thin, he could push his fingers into his abdomen and feel his spine. He became very weak and was close to death when he had the realization of what is now called 'The Middle Way'. He understood that the path to truth does not come through extremes, but through finding a path of balance and harmony.

He then gave up fasting and devoted himself to meditation. One full-moon evening, he was sitting under a Bo Tree and vowed to stay there until he understood the inner mysteries of the universe. Siddhartha's meditation deepened through the night and as Venus rose in the morning sky, he achieved 'The Great Awakening' and from that moment on he was Siddhartha no more, but had become Buddha.

This 3rd-century carving entitled The Great Departure *shows Prince Siddhartha with his horse Kanthaka leaving his noble life in search of truth.*

In order to discover the deepest truths, one must let go of attachment to material things and walk a simpler path.

He founded an order of monks and over the next 45 years devoted nine months of each year to public speaking and private teaching and three months to contemplation with his monks.

Although regarded as a religion, Buddhism does not focus practice on the worship of God as a separate being, but on the realization of one's own divinity. It is that 'knowing of oneself' on which Buddhism is founded. Indeed the name, 'Buddha', can be translated as 'to know' or 'to awaken'. Buddha's teachings have adapted themselves to every country where they have travelled and when Buddhism came to China, it evolved into Zen, teaching the art of awakening through meditation. Fundamentally though, despite adaptation, Zen has at its core the teachings of Buddha.

THE FOUR NOBLE TRUTHS

As a result of his enlightenment, Buddha came to a realization of Four Noble Truths. These are as relevant in Zen practice as in other forms of Buddhism for all Zen Masters began their paths with the understanding of the Four Noble Truths.

1 The Existence of Suffering

The first Noble Truth is that life is full of suffering for as Siddhartha travelled, everywhere he went, he saw pain and suffering amongst the people. Although we all seek happiness, so often it is fleeting and indeed what makes us happy does not often last. When we are hungry, eating good food makes us feel happier. But if we ate beyond our fill we would soon fall into the suffering of stomach pain; so to continue feeling happy we stop eating. Too much or too little food leads us to suffering making our happiness very fragile. So it is with all of life; we seek happiness, grasp it and then lose it all too quickly. Suffering, however, is present with us all the time. Sometimes we do not notice it, especially during moments of happiness, but it is with us none the same. This may at first seem rather pessimistic, but it is what drives us towards understanding the second Noble Truth.

'Through perseverance,
vigilance and self-restraint,
a wise person creates a safe
harbour for herself, that no
storm can overwhelm.'

BUDDHA

2 The Causes of Suffering

The second Noble Truth is that there is a cause to our suffering. Our resistance to accepting situations we find ourselves in causes this suffering. We suffer either because things we desire are denied us or because things we dislike manifest in our lives. For instance, a lover may 'suffer' heartache when their mate is away from them, especially if it is for a long time. Equally, a person may suffer when they have an illness that produces symptoms they dislike. The second truth also teaches that it is only our attachment to things and desires that causes us to suffer.

3 The Cessation of the Causes of Suffering

The third Noble Truth teaches that the source of this suffering can be removed. By letting go of our attachments our suffering comes to an end. We cause ourselves to suffer, albeit often at a subconscious level, by choosing to hold on to the past. We hold on to anger, resentment, painful memories or sentimentality. Once we let go, we become free.

This painting, Life of Buddha, *from the Temple of Yongju, Suwon, South Korea shows Siddhartha witnessing death, suffering and a monk meditating.*

4 The Path that Leads to the Cessation of the Causes of Suffering

The fourth Noble Truth speaks of a path we can follow that has the potential to remove all sources of suffering. Buddha called this path, 'The Eightfold Path' and 'The Middle Way'. The Middle Way refers to walking between extremes rather than at them and is the main goal of a Zen disciple. In modern sensorial living, we are forever seeking more extreme ways to give ourselves pleasure, be it through drugs, alcohol, food, shopping or other forms of materialism. The Middle Way teaches 'everything in moderation'. Do not eat too much, sleep too much, work too much or play too much. One extreme always leads to its opposite – happiness to sadness, ecstasy to insanity, love to hatred and tolerance to anger. Too much of anything can put you on a road to ultimate suffering.

Buddha saw the Four Noble Truths as a form of medicine used to treat the most fundamental human illness, which is suffering. Zen has modified the prescription to make this medicine available to anyone who wishes to take it, regardless of lifestyle, class, gender or religion.

THE EIGHTFOLD PATH

Zen disciples seek to walk what Buddha called 'The Middle Way' which he also described as 'The Eightfold Path'. The Eightfold Path refers to eight areas of our lives that deserve our attention if we are to break free of suffering. These eight areas come under three subheadings, wisdom, morality and calming concentration. It is important to understand that all eight areas need to be developed simultaneously and not in a linear way. This is because each area helps in the cultivation of the other seven areas, so to ignore one or more areas is to dilute the experience of all eight.

The Eightfold Path is as follows:

- Right View

- Right Intent or Wisdom

- Right Speech

- Right Action

- Right Livelihood

- Right Effort or Morality

- Mindfulness

- Concentration or Calming concentration

Right View comes through the proper understanding of Buddha's teachings. It involves breaking through the illusions of the ego, which divides and separates everything, and realizing the unity of all creation. Right View is more than being open, it is being aware that we create our perspective via our five senses, which give us only a very limited view of what is being presented to us. When someone is speaking to us, most people cannot tell whether it is truth or lies they are hearing. Only someone who is open to both and makes no judgements about either as good and bad or right and wrong can hope to perceive the truth. Likewise, our eyes, nose, taste and touch are all highly unreliable for taking in the big picture. The world is full of electromagnetic waves; they bombard us every day and yet we are totally unaware of this. Does that mean they don't exist? Right View leads us to looking at things in a way that is deeper. It

challenges us to look beneath the surface and to realize that our experiences are fleeting. This in turn may lead us to resolve to understand the nature of things in a deeper, more lasting way.

Right Intent initially arises from making a decision, both intellectually and emotionally, to follow a path towards a deeper understanding of Self. From this comes an inner determination to meet and resolve those old habits and character traits that lead us into separation and suffering. Right Intent is the will to carry out the correct action. In order to move forward with Right Intent, you must be free of all selfish motives and desires because they inevitably lead to negative emotions such as fear, anger, guilt and greed from which no Right Action can arise.

Right Speech is about developing a true awareness of what we say and how we say it. Words are powerful and correct communication is extremely important in all aspects of our lives. The root of most arguments lies in misunderstanding and miscommunication. According to Buddhist teaching there are four elements to Right Speech. The first is abstaining from telling lies and cultivating truthful speech. The second is abstaining from malicious or slanderous speech and cultivating speech that builds friendship and trust. The third is abstaining from shouting, insulting or being sarcastic and cultivating

Meditation is at the core of Buddhist practice but Buddha taught that it is only one part of the Eightfold Path to enlightenment.

courteous, respectful speech. The fourth is abstaining from idle chatter and gossip and cultivating speech that is meaningful and valuable. Right Speech presents such a challenge that Zen teaches its understanding through long periods of silence.

Right Action means taking full and personal responsibility for all your actions no matter how minor. If we cultivate the positive emotions of generosity, love, compassion and understanding our actions will reflect these. Such skilful actions unite people, break down divisions and have a quality that promotes both personal and universal good. Buddha taught that all beings have buddhanature (the innate potential in all human beings to become a Buddha) so we need to be mindful of not only how we treat our fellow human beings but all the inhabitants of this wonderfully rich and diverse planet we live on.

These statues in Thailand show four Buddhas in the classic half-lotus meditation pose as used in Zen meditation.

Lay Buddhists often practise five precepts to Right Action. These are not killing, not taking that which is not given, not misusing the senses, not lying and not misusing intoxicants. Buddhist monks and nuns practise many more precepts but even these five offer us all a challenge if we think deeply enough about them. Not killing means ants, wasps, flies and all other insects not only other humans. Not taking that which is not given is more than just not stealing, it also means, for example, not taking the money you find dropped in the street. Not misusing the senses means not following roads of pure sensorial pleasure and includes being mindful about what you taste, look at (including television and newspapers) and listen to.

Right Livelihood means that doing work that does not harm the environment at large, our fellow human beings or ourselves. This is a particular challenge for many people in the West as the whole Western economy is run on peoples' desire to have material wealth regardless of the cost. Profit is all too often placed above the needs of individuals and the

long-term needs of the planet. To work purely for financial gain is a path towards misery and suffering. Life should be endlessly fulfilling and this means that you need to both enjoy your work and be able to practise all aspects of your spiritual path while doing it. There are many jobs that are ethical and many more companies are becoming aware of their need to act responsibly to both their employees and the environment at large.

Right Effort means working only for good. This requires one to exorcise unhealthy and unnatural states of being such as desire, envy and delusion, whilst cultivating wholesome states of being such as understanding, generosity, compassion, love and kindness. Effort is the energy behind our actions brought into being by our intent. If the energy behind our actions is selfish, no matter how good those actions may be, they will still cause suffering either to ourselves or others. Likewise it is foolish to compromise our own happiness to help others, yet so many people do this thinking that they are acting

Throughout Asia there are many huge and significant statues of Buddha such as this one found in the Datong-Yunguan Buddhist caves in China.

unselfishly. If you cannot do something with joy and love in your heart, then you are not truly practising Right Effort.

Right Mindfulness is one of the truly liberating aspects of Buddhist and particularly Zen practice as it teaches one to live in the present. As we shall see, it is a powerful and enlightening skill that has endless positive applications in daily life. Right Concentration is achieved only when the other seven points of the Eightfold Path are balanced and in place. It is learned through the art of meditation, which in Zen is called *zazen*. There is no short cut to achieving Right Concentration. It comes only through diligent and patient practice that is at the heart of the Zen path. To choose to walk a Zen path is a truly life-changing decision.

WHAT IS ZEN?

Ask a Zen master the question 'What is Zen?' and his answer is unlikely to start with 'Zen is…'. In all likelihood, he will say something like, 'Go and drink some tea'. This is because to ask such a question is to take a step away from the truth of what Zen really is. Zen was created in China about one thousand years after the birth of Buddhism at a time when most Buddhist traditions extolled the virtues of studying the scriptures as a means to attaining enlightenment. Zen, however, holds that the truth is not to be found within the scriptures, but in a person's own heart. Through meditation and self-mastery, Zen students seek to find the truth within themselves. This truth does not reveal itself through the intellectual mind with its endless questions, but arises from the heart and can do so only when the mind stops questioning.

To understand Zen is to understand life itself. Zen is about being present in the moment and perceiving the wonder and beauty of that moment whatever it is like. To walk a Zen path is to do everything with grace and beauty from opening a door, making tea and washing to writing poetry, painting, arranging flowers and performing martial arts. Even the most mundane of tasks takes on new and wonderful perspectives when approached in a Zen manner. To watch a Zen master go through his daily life is to watch someone act with grace, love, humility and honour in everything they do. It is like watching the most beautiful ballet or hearing the most beautiful piece of music.

Zen teaches that we are all living in a dream, a dream called 'delusion'. We think that external events dictate whether we are happy or sad, we live in fear of imagined future scenarios and carry the pain of the past on our shoulders like a heavy sack. Zen extols us to 'wake up' and realize the truth of our own divinity. We are each divine and have the power within us to make our own reality. When we truly see our own buddhanature, we see it reflected back to us in everything we encounter. Life, instead of being a roller coaster of emotional highs and lows, becomes a steady and unfolding experience of divine beauty. We live in the most incredible world, filled with marvels and wonders, yet so often all we perceive is pain and suffering. But we base these perceptions on what we hold within us. If we hold pain and suffering within us, what we see outside of us is nothing more or less than the reflection of that pain. If we learn to let go of our pain, we begin to see beyond the suffering of the world and into its true divine beauty. This is the beginning of an understanding of the power of Zen.

> 'Delusion is dreaming;
> enlightenment is
> awakening.'
>
> P'U-AN

To become a Buddhist monk is a serious decision but does not mean choosing a life without fun and laughter as these novice monks show.

With Zen even the simple act of making tea has the potential to bring about enlightenment if approached with honour, humility and respect.

THE HISTORY AND DEVELOPMENT OF ZEN

'Zen is not thought, the path has no achievement…you transcend seeing and hearing, get rid of all dependence, and ride at leisure on top of sound and form, mastering that which startles the crowd.'

HUAI-T'ANG

THE GENESIS OF ZEN

After his enlightening experience under the Bo tree, Buddha devoted himself to spreading his teachings to all who would listen. He attracted a great many followers and those who felt the call to devote the rest of their lives to following this path were ordained as monks and nuns. He died around the age of eighty from food poisoning. His final words to his disciples were, 'Impermanent are all created things. Strive on with awareness… 'Buddha left behind a wealth of teachings and his followers spread the word of his teachings and methods across India and then into the bordering countries. By the 1st century CE Buddhism had reached China where it met the philosophies of Confucianism and Taoism and found much common ground. Over the next few centuries all the Buddhist texts were translated into Chinese and most Chinese Buddhists approached study in a very scholastic manner.

This Japanese scroll depiciting the death of Buddha reminds us of the impermanence of all created things.

In around 479 CE, an Indian monk named Bodhidharma arrived in China and challenged the existing Buddhist practices which he felt over-emphasized scholarly study. He extolled a path of simple directness designed to wake up disciples from the dreams of delusions into an appreciation of the here and now. The emphasis was not on the study of sacred texts but on meditation.

From China, Zen Buddhism spread to Korea, Japan and Vietnam and much later on to Europe and America. Although Zen has developed differently in different countries, all Zen practice has sitting meditation, known as *zazen*, as its main feature and is designed to awaken you to your true nature. Zen actually means meditation. It originates from the Sanskrit word Dhyana, which means the meditative state achieved in the Buddhist tradition. When Buddhism arrived in China, Dhyana was transliterated as Chan and this character is pronounced Son in Korea and Zen in Japan. Although the Zen tradition did not emerge until centuries after his death, Buddha is credited as the true originator of Zen thought. The following episode from the Buddha's teaching is most often cited as the first Zen story.

The First Zen Story

Buddha was staying at a place called Vulture Park sharing his teaching each day with his many followers. One morning he arrived to find twelve hundred monks, nuns and lay people seated, waiting to listen to his words of wisdom. Buddha sat before them in silence. For a long time he just sat there quietly and his followers sat in silence waiting and wondering. Finally he held up a flower, silently displaying it to the crowd. Nobody understood this gesture except Mahakasyapa, one of his monk disciples, who smiled, having understood that no words could be a substitute for the perfect beauty of a flower. Buddha smiled back saying, 'Here is the true Way and I transmit it to you.'

MAHAYANA: THE ORIGIN OF ZEN

After Buddha's death, Theravada Buddhism became the dominant form focussing primarily on meditation and concentration. It centred on monastic life with extended times spent in meditation. This made it relatively inaccessible to a majority of ordinary people; so in the 1st century CE, a new movement began in Buddhism, one that sought to reformulate the teaching of Buddha to encompass a greater number of people. This new form of Buddhism was called Mahayana or 'the Greater Vehicle' since it could accommodate people from all walks of life. The Mahayanists did not see themselves as creating a new form of Buddhism, but rather reclaiming the original teachings of Buddha.

One of the early Mahayanist schools was called the Yogacara School (yoga means meditation). The Yogacaras believed that the ultimate truth could not be found in studying the Dharmas (scriptures) as these were only relative truths subject to change and re-interpretation. They believed that the ultimate truth could only arise from within through meditation. They divided truth into three categories, Illusory Truth, Empirical Truth and Absolute Truth. This can be seen in the following example. You are walking along a road when, out of the corner of your eye you see what you think is a coiled snake. On closer examination you realize that actually what you are seeing is a coiled rope. Your first impression is an example of Illusory Truth and your second an example of Empirical Truth. If you sat and meditated on the rope you would perceive that it is made up of many individual strands, which themselves are made up of smaller pieces of material (which we call protons, electrons and neutrons) and ultimately you would realize that it is actually made up of pure energy appearing as form – this is Absolute Truth. It was from this kind of thinking that many of the Zen principles arose.

All Zen schools belong to the Mahayana tradition of Buddhism, a tradition that encompasses many different approaches and thus can appeal to a wide variety of people. Zen is especially noted for being a form of Buddhism not only for monks and nuns but also for lay people. Zen teaches that enlightenment is available to anyone, regardless of age, sex, social position or knowledge. It also teaches that enlightenment can come at any time and under any circumstance. This makes Zen particularly appealing to Westerners as it allows them to walk a Zen path whilst living as part of normal society. Zen teachings are applicable to all aspects of life and therefore one can practise Zen in any and all circumstances, from

'If a man speaks or acts with a pure mind,
joy follows him as his own shadow.'

BUDDHA

walking to driving a car, from hanging out the washing to performing great works of creativity. Zen wisdom is a thread that weaves through the diverse experiences of human life giving them new meaning and purpose.

One of the main innovations of Mahayana Buddhism that has been taken forward by Zen is the idea of the bodhisattva. The bodhisattva or 'being of wisdom' arose in the Mahayana tradition as a way to explain the nature of Buddha's earlier lives. Before Buddha incarnated in his final life as Siddhartha, it is believed that he spent many lives as a bodhisattva, an apprentice buddha so to speak. During these lives he performed great acts of compassion, generosity and kindness towards his fellow men and it was these lives of humble service that ultimately enabled him to achieve Buddhahood. There emerged many writings about Buddha's previous lives called the *Jataka* or 'Birth Stories'.

This in turn led to an understanding that perhaps a second or even a third Buddha might return to Earth, hence the doctrine of the Maitreya, or 'Future Buddha' arose. This doctrine believes that a second Buddha would come to Earth to purify the world and that if this were so, this Buddha was already a bodhisattva, coming to Earth many times in many lives on his or her journey towards Buddhahood. This means that someone on Earth today is the Maitreya. It could be a child playing, the waitress serving you dinner, your mother, father, brother, sister or even you!

This Japanese statue of Yakushi, the Medicine Buddha embodies the idea that the root of all illness begins in the mind.

BODHIDHARMA:
THE FOUNDER OF ZEN

Bodhidharma was a semi-legendary monk who was born in what is now southern
India around 440 CE. At about the age of 35 he undertook the long journey to China
to broaden his vision of Buddhism. He visited various Chinese monasteries but
wherever he went he found the monks were preoccupied with scholastic studies of
ancient texts.

In 520 CE Bodhidharma reached southern China
and was invited to an audience with Emperor Wu
of the Liang dynasty. The emperor asked him, 'How
much merit have you accumulated through
building temples and giving generous offerings to
monasteries?' To which Bodhidharma replied, 'None
at all.' This perplexed the emperor so he asked, 'Well,
what is the highest teaching of Buddhism?' 'Vast
emptiness,' was the bewildering reply. The emperor

was now losing patience and said, 'Who do you think
you are?' to which Bodhidharma replied, 'I do not
know.' At this the Emperor banished Bodhidharma
from the court and it is said that he then spent the
next seven years sat in meditation 'listening to the
ants scream.'

After this Bodhidharma crossed the Yangtze River
and made his way to the now famous Shaolin
Temple. Here the monks spent most of their time

translating Sanskrit texts into Chinese, working in shifts both day and night. It is said that the abbot refused him permission to live in the monastery for fear that his teachings, especially that the learning from books was unnecessary, might upset the status quo of the temple. After this there are several stories that tell of how Bodhidarma finally gained entry into the temple. One tale tells that he sat for the next nine years facing the wall of the temple, meditating and that he burnt holes in the wall just by staring at it. Another says that he went to a nearby cave to meditate to prove that 'the highest form of wisdom is not attained through the performance of orthodox rituals nor through the translation and study of Sanskrit texts.' According to this version of the story the monks from the temple started coming to visit this enigmatic sage and although they sought to question him, he remained always in silent meditation.

Eventually the abbot relented and Bodhidharma entered the monastery as the first patriarch of Chan (Zen). Once inside he found the monks to be in a poor physical state due to their life of study spent copying ancient texts. To remedy this he taught them a series of martial exercises (probably of Taoist origin), which later became the foundation of the Shaolin School of Kung Fu. He taught two forms of exercises, the first was the Yi-Jin-Jing, a series of twelve Qigong (energy building) exercises to strengthen muscles and nerves. The second was the Xi-Sui-Jing, a series of internal and external exercises for meditation and to strengthen the bone marrow. The monks practised these exercises daily and soon grew in both strength and vitality. Through this Bodhidharma proved that on the earthly plane the spirit and body are inseparable and that only through strengthening both can one reach *Satori* (enlightenment).

Not only is Bodhidharma recognized as the founder of Zen, he is also credited as the father of Kung Fu and the bringer of tea to China. This latter achievement comes from a story that tells of how he was having problems sustaining long periods of

Bodhidharma is regarded as the founder of both Zen Buddhism and Kung Fu. He taught the importance of respecting the body, mind and spirit.

meditation due to falling asleep. To remedy this he cut off his eyelids and tea bushes sprung up from the place where his eyelids fell. The following quotation, attributed to Bodhidharma, is often cited as a representation of the true spirit of Zen:

A special tradition outside of the scriptures
with no dependence upon words or letters;
Directly it points to the heart of man,
Seeing into one's own nature,
One attains Buddhahood.

Shaolin Buddhist monks practising Kung Fu at the Pagoda Forest near the Shaolin monastery in Henan Province, China.

THE CHINESE CHAN

Bodhidharma's successor as patriarch of Zen was a monk called Huiko (c.485–c.553 CE). According to one story Huiko visited Bodhidharma at Shaolin repeatedly requesting teaching but was always met with silence. Eventually, to attract the master's attention and to show the depth of his intent, Huiko took hold of a sword and cut off his left arm. Bodhidharma rewarded this dramatic act by immediately agreeing to talk with the monk.

Master Hsuyun travelled extensively throughout China spreading the teachings of Chan (Zen) Buddhism and most modern Chan masters studied under him.

'Your disciple's soul is not at peace,' cried Huiko, 'I beg you master, give it rest.'

Bodhidharma replied, 'Bring your soul to me and I will give it rest.'

Huiko sat for a long time searching for his soul and eventually said, 'Master, I have searched for my soul but can find no trace of it.'

'See,' exclaimed Bodhidharma, 'I have put it to rest once and for all.'

This conversation resulted in the awakening of Huiko.

After Huiko, Zen transmission went on to Sengtsan (origins unknown, d.606 CE), then Taohsin (580–651 CE) followed by Hungjen (600–674 CE) who had many disciples and lived in a monastery on Mount Huang Mei. By the middle of the 8th century there were at least seven different Chan schools with two of them, the Northern and Southern schools, engaged in an often acrimonious debate about matters of doctrine that lasted for several decades. The Northern school held that enlightenment arose through gradual practice whereas the Southern school favoured the idea of sudden enlightenment.

From this time there emerged what are now called 'The Five Houses of Classical Zen', each with its own style of practice.

The House of Kuei-Yang is said to have favoured an active path with rules such as, 'A day without work, a day without food.' In this school a student was expected to respond to his master's questions with deeds rather than words.

The Fa-yen house was founded by renowned Zen master Fa-yen who was said to have utilized the technique of repeating the same word or phrase to his students in response to any question they asked. He is said to have had over a thousand disciples and more than sixty enlightened successors.

The third house was named after Zen master Yun-men, who was by all accounts a prolific teacher. However, he forbade his disciples from writing down his own words as he felt that to do so would be at the expense of their direct experience of reality. One of his long serving disciples, however, surreptitiously recorded his words on a robe made of paper (worn by monks to remind them of the impermanence of things) and many of his teachings are still studied today.

The House of Lin-Chi developed the use of shock tactics to stimulate the direct experience of the moment outside of conventional thought patterns and although it went into decline it was later revived and by the middle of the 11th century it had established itself as one of the most important schools. It is one of only two houses that continue to flourish today. Master Lin-Chi's use of shock tactics, including shouting at and hitting his students, is well documented. Once a monk asked him, 'What is the fundamental principle of the Buddha's teaching?' Master Lin-Chi replied with a shout. The monk responded with a low bow. 'As an opponent in debate, this young monk is rather good,' said Master Lin-Chi.

The House of Tsao-Tung, which also survives today, is particularly known for a teaching technique called 'The Five Ranks'. It advocated the unifying of the relative world (ordinary experience) with the absolute world (enlightened experience) and developed the practice of 'just sitting' without doing anything.

The Life of a Chan Monk

A typical Chan monastery of the 8th century CE was divided into separate buildings as follows: the Dharma hall for lectures, the Buddha hall for ceremonies and the monks' hall for meditation, eating and sleeping. These buildings were usually located in a row leading up the side of a hill or mountain and surrounded by a high wall. The monks would work in the surrounding fields and forests, cook and clean or take on administrative duties. The rest of their time was devoted to meditation, listening to lectures about Buddhist doctrine and philosophy or performing ceremonies. Monks would often move from temple to temple, receiving teachings from many different masters. It was not unknown for a monk to study with 50 or more different masters representing all the five houses as well as other Zen traditions. There were many diverse meditation practices and it appears there was much experimentation with these practices during the 8th century although there is little known about the specifics of this experimentation.

During the Sung period (960–1279 CE), Zen in China continued to thrive and expand whilst most other forms of Buddhism were declining. Taoism and the resurgence of Confucianism (Neo-Confucianism) both contributed to this decline and by the end of the Sung dynasty only the Chan and Pure Land schools of Buddhism had any real following in China. Marxism in the 20th century further contributed to the decline of Buddhism in China. Paradoxically the Marxist government formed the Chinese Buddhist Association whilst discouraging the practice of Buddhism even within the association itself. Communism and the Cultural Revolution dealt further blows to an already much weakened remnant of Buddhism with temples sacked and nuns and monks heavily persecuted by the Red Guards.

Since 1976 however, China has allowed access to the West once more and there is a growing tolerance towards Buddhism these days in China. Temples are being rebuilt and although religion is not encouraged, those wishing to practise Buddhism are now being allowed to do so. Zen training is once again taking place in China with monks and nuns being allowed to live a traditional Zen way of life once more. Most modern Chinese masters were followers of Master Hsuyun (1840–1959), a master renowned for his longevity and the many pilgrimages that he took all over China and even to India. It is doubtful that Zen will ever become great once more in China but the very fact that it is still being practised there at all is a testament to its enduring wisdom and appeal.

'Looking into a precious mirror,
Form and reflection beholding each other:
You are not it;
It is you.'

TUNG-SHAN OF THE HOUSE OF TSAO-TUNG

THE KOREAN SON

Buddhism entered Korea from China in 372 CE. Prior to this shamanism was the indigenous religion and held three spirits in particular reverence: Sanshin, the mountain spirit who is usually depicted as an old man with a tiger at his feet; Toksong, or the Recluse; and Ch'ilsong (the spirit of the seven stars, the Big Dipper). Buddhism was not seen to conflict with these beliefs and even today in most Korean Buddhist temples there are shrines to these three spirits.

In the 4th century CE Korea was divided into three kingdoms, Koguryo, Paekje and Shilla. In 372 CE, a monk was invited from China to visit the northern kingdom of Koguryo by the ruling royal family. He brought Buddhist texts and statues and Buddhist beliefs were quickly accepted there as they had much in common with the indigenous shamanistic beliefs. In 384 CE Buddhism spread to the south-western kingdom of Paekje, where it was likewise embraced. Shilla though, was much more reluctant to embrace Buddhism until the martyrdom of Ichiadon in 527 CE. Ichiadon, a high-ranking court official, announced to King Pophung (514–540 CE) that he had become a Buddhist, whereupon the king ordered his immediate execution. When Ichiadon was beheaded, milk flowed out instead of blood and this miracle led to

the king's conversion. In 668 CE Shilla conquered the other kingdoms and Buddhism became the central religious force.

One master in particular, Won-hyo (617–686 CE), is credited with bringing the various schools and doctrines of Korean Buddhism together in a more unified approach. His awakening came when he was a young man in search of a teacher. Won-hyo and his close friend Ui-sang set out to China to study at the monasteries there. On the way, Won-hyo awoke one night with a tremendous thirst and searching around him found a bowl containing delicious water, which he drank. With his thirst quenched he returned to sleep. In the morning, when he awoke, he found that the vessel was in fact a shattered human skull and the water within it stagnant. He was shocked and disgusted but then in that moment he realized that 'thinking makes good and bad' and that everything depends on the mind. Zen likewise teaches us to let go of our perceptions of good and bad and to 'just be in the moment'.

It was towards the end of the Unified Shilla Period (668–935 CE) that the Chan school of Buddhist thought was first introduced to Korea and soon nine new schools emerged known as the Nine Mountains of Son. Buddhism continued as the national religion during the Koryo Dynasty (935–1392 CE) with kings establishing new temples and shrines throughout the country. The nine schools of Son were unified by Master Taego (1301–1382) towards the end of the Koryo Dynasty under the name Chogye and this has remained the primary Son sect to this day. The Choson Dynasty (1392–1910) adopted Neo-Confucianism, which led to the persecution of Buddhists and the destruction of many temples. After liberation in 1945, many men and women were ordained and more recently new temples have been built in many of the major towns providing programmes for all people and ages, teaching meditation and studying Buddhist texts. Today about half the Korean population is Buddhist with much of the rest of the country adopting a Buddhist-type view of life and the after-life.

One characteristic of Korean monastic Zen is that there is total equality between monks and nuns with both sharing the same teachings, practices and positions. In order to be ordained as either a monk or nun, one has to complete a postulant period of up to a year or more, then become a novice and only at a later time will one become fully ordained. This is then followed by three to four years of studying sutras and Zen texts before one is finally allowed to enter a Zen hall to practise meditation. Today many Westerners travel to Korea to study Zen in Korean monasteries.

'Wherever we go, keep harmony with others and help the poor;
Real 'I' is a pure and clear thing originally.'

HYE AM SUNIM: RESIDENT MASTER
OF HAE IN-SA TEMPLE, KOREA

Today there are many magnificent Buddhist temples in Korea such as the Hwaomsa Temple, Jirisan National Park, South Korea.

THE JAPANESE ZEN

Buddhism arrived in Japan from Korea in 538 CE when the ruler of Paekje, a small state in the southwest of Korea that was at war with a neighbouring state, sent a delegation to Japan seeking support. The ambassadors brought with them Buddhist statues and scriptures to present to Emperor Kimmei. The emperor was impressed with this new religion and over the next few decades Buddhism began to establish itself and with the patronage of Prince Shotoku (574–622 CE) it became the state religion. Although Prince Shotoku did not found a school of Buddhism nor did he become a priest, he is regarded as the founder of Japanese Buddhism.

Zen was introduced in Japan as early as the 7th century but did not establish itself until much later. It was during the Kamakura period (1192–1333) that Zen rose to prominence due largely to the work of two monks, Eisai and Dogen. Eisai (1141–1215) is considered the founder of Japanese Zen and began his spiritual life as a Tendai monk. The Tendai School sought to harmonize all Buddhist teachings and is based on the Lotus Sutra, a scripture that contains many of the fundamental teachings of Mahayana Buddhism. Eisai travelled to China where he was greatly influenced by the teachings of the Lin-Chi school of Chan (Zen). In Japan this became known as the Rinzai School.

In 1191 Eisai returned from China and finding that his new understandings brought him into conflict with the Tendai School, established the first Rinzai sect teaching strict meditation based on the use of koans. Eisai also taught that Zen should defend the state and allowed the observance of ceremonial rules appealing to the warrior class and winning him favour with the Shoguns. This led to Zen having great influence upon the martial arts of archery and swordsmanship as well as other arts such as poetry, flower-arranging and tea, all of which stress the importance of grace and spontaneity. The Shogun Minamoto Yoriie, a keen supporter of Rinzai Zen's strictness and discipline, nominated Eisai as abbot of Kennin-ji monastery in Kyoto in 1204, thus assuring the further establishment of Zen teachings in Japan.

Dogen (1200–1253) was born into a family of nobility and by the age of seven learned the lesson of the transitory nature of life with the deaths of his father and mother. At 13 he was ordained as a monk and began studying the Buddhist scriptures at the monastery on Mount Hiei. However, he was unable to find the answer to a fundamental question: 'If all beings originally possess buddhanature, why does one need to engage in practices to realize it?'

In 1223 he travelled to China and spent the next four years studying at various Zen monasteries and temples. Initially he studied koans but felt these placed too much emphasis on paradoxical actions and words and so went to study with Zen Master Juching (1163–1228). Master Juching shunned fame and fortune preferring a path of simplicity and of 'letting go of both mind and body.' He taught a form of meditation which involved 'just sitting', not trying to answer riddles nor trying to gain enlightenment and it was through this practice that Dogen himself became enlightened.

In 1227 Dogen returned to Japan and formed the Soto School of Zen and over the next few years he devoted himself to spreading the word of Zen and to writing what are now regarded as among the most important of Japanese Zen works. His chief work,

Zen greatly influenced all cultural life in Japan, including architecture. This can be seen in the simple lines and form of the Golden Temple pictured here.

Shobogenzo – Treasury of the True Dharma Eye, took more than 20 years to write and contains 95 chapters of his elaboration on Buddhist principles. In 1243 he moved to the Echizen province and founded the temple of Eihei-ji northwest of Nagoya, which remains to this day one of the main monasteries of the Soto Zen School.

Dogen taught *shikan taza*, Zazen sitting meditation without any effort being directed towards enlightenment. However, unlike his Chinese counterparts, he also emphasized the need to study the scriptures and strongly criticized those who did not. He also put great emphasis on correct posture during meditation and asserted that sitting still was enlightenment itself. After his death in 1253, Dogen was all but forgotten, even by his own school and it was not until the 1800s that he was rediscovered and his great wisdom was once more studied.

This painting depicts Zen Master Dogen practising calligraphy while his Buddhist monks sit in Zen meditation in Bukkokuji Monastery, Japan.

After Dogen's death Japan went through a time of great political turmoil and upheaval with the Rinzai sect fairing much better than the Soto sect. During the latter part of the 14th century, arts and scholarship flourished in the five Zen monasteries of Kyoto under the patronage of the shogun Ashikaga Yoshimitsu and Zen monks were given special protection and often served as political advisors. During the 15th and 16th centuries the Zen schools degenerated and it was only at the beginning of the Tokugawa Period (1603–1867) that Zen tradition once again saw a revival. During this time the Zen arts continued to grow and expand and some remarkable artists emerged including architects, playwrights and poets.

Several eminent Zen masters emerged during this period including Bankei (1622–1693) who simply taught that in order to gain enlightenment one had only to 'listen to the unborn Buddha-heart' and Hakuin (1686–1769) who revitalized the Rinzai School and from whom all modern Rinzai masters trace descent. He is the author of the famous koan,

'What is the sound of one hand clapping?' Hakuin advocated balancing meditation with work saying 'For penetrating to the depths of one's true nature…nothing can surpass meditation in the midst of activity.' This is an important aspect of Zen practice today, allowing one to live Zen in all aspects of life.

In 1868 there was a *coup d'état* in Japan that restored imperial rule and established Shintoism as the state religion. The imperial powers sought to weaken Buddhism by encouraging monks to marry and eat meat. Today most Zen monks are married and many have inherited a family temple from their families. They often train for only two or three years at a formal Zen monastery before returning to their own family temples and acting as priests to their local community.

Zen thought was introduced to the West by the writings of D.T. Suzuki (1870–1966). Suzuki studied in his youth under Zen Master Soen and under Soen's guidance gained the experience of Satori (sudden enlightenment). He spent 13 years in the United States from 1897 until 1909 working as a magazine editor and first attracted interest by a translation he wrote

> *'If you seek to travel the way of Buddhas and Zen masters, then expect nothing, seek nothing and grasp nothing.'*
>
> DOGEN

entitled 'The Discourse on the Awakening of Faith in the Mahayana' (1900). He spent the latter part of his life travelling mainly throughout Japan and the United States teaching and lecturing about Buddhism and especially Zen. Even wider interest in Zen Buddhism blossomed after the Second World War with centres established throughout Europe and the United States. A great many writers produced translations or volumes of their own extolling the virtues of this simple approach to life and self-discovery.

ZEN IN AMERICA

The West's first encounters with Zen involved Western missionaries in China and Japan trying to 'convert' Zen Buddhists to Christianity. This was more a case of missionaries trying to change the thinking of Buddhists rather than looking at their own thinking. The first real Western encounter with Zen wisdom came in 1893 when Zen Master Soen was invited to speak at the world's Parliament of Religions in Chicago. Afterwards he was asked if he could help make Buddhist texts more available to the West through translation and he recommended one of his students, Daisetz Teitaro Suzuki for the job. D.T. Suzuki became one of the foremost writers on Zen in the West, influencing and inspiring a great many Western writers including Carl Jung, Aldous Huxley and Allen Ginsberg. Zen has further been popularized and made more accessible to the West by writers such as Alan Watts and Thomas Cleary.

In 1905 Master Soen returned to America bringing with him his disciple Nyogen Senzaki (1876–1958), who became the first Zen monk to settle in America. He began teaching Zen meditation in various public halls and his success encouraged other monks to come over to teach. At this time there were a great number of Asian immigrants going to America and this further attracted Zen monks over to serve their spiritual needs as well as teaching Westerners. One of them was Taizan Maezumi Roshi, who in 1967 founded the Zen Center of Los Angeles specifically for the training of Westerners. Two years later in 1969, Shunryu Suzuki, the author of *Zen Mind, Beginners Mind* set up the San Francisco Zen Center which went on to initiate many new projects including a farm training centre, a mountain retreat centre and a Buddhist Hospice movement. From here, Zen Buddhism spread across America and by 1990 there were some 200 Zen centres in the United States and ten years after that this figure had more than doubled.

The Rochester Zen Center's history begins at the Nuremberg and Tokyo War Crimes Trials at the close of World War II. Philip Kapleau (1912–2004) was a court reporter at the trials and listening day after day to horrific testimonies caused him to begin a search

to try to make sense of all he had witnessed. This led him in 1953 to a Zen monastery in Japan and for the next 13 years he trained first under Harada-Roshi and then his successor Yasutami-Roshi. He published his experiences in the now classic Western Zen book *The Three Pillars of Zen*. In March of 1966, he was invited to come to Rochester and work with a meditation group, and in June the Zen Meditation Center came into being with a membership of 22.

Since then the centre has thrived and grown, establishing affiliated centres throughout America as well as in Canada, Mexico, Costa Rica and Europe. It follows a tradition of integrated Zen, teaching elements from both the Rinzai and Soto schools. The centre is designed to accommodate full-time students and so encourages only serious practitioners to join, although it also runs monthly one-day introductory workshops for those contemplating becoming members. In 1986 Roshi Kapleau retired passing his directorship on to Sensei Bodhin Kjolhede. He continued to be actively involved in the centre and remained living there until his death on 6 May 2004 from complications of Parkinson's disease. He died a beautiful and peaceful death in the sunlit garden of the Zen Center surrounded by his students, family and friends.

The Rochester Zen Center is one of the oldest Buddhist
communities in the United States and offers authentic Zen
training in a Western context.

Roshi Kapleau was a deeply spiritual man with a joy for living
that was clearly visible to all who met him.

ZEN IN THE MODERN WORLD

Since the 1960s the interest in Zen Buddhism in the West has steadily grown with meditation centres and teaching schools being set up all over the world including New Zealand and Australia, throughout Europe, South Africa and the Americas. Some are simply buildings where like-minded people can meet to practise Zen meditation and share teachings; others are retreats whilst some are full-time monasteries where Westerners can devote themselves to a full monastic life in much the same way as in Asia. Most Western Zen Buddhists are not monastic, however.

One of the major developments in Western Zen is in the role of women. In Japan, with its highly patriarchal traditions, there are still few nuns or female priests and relatively few places where women can train. In the West it is often women who have found it easier to take on the deeper teachings of Zen and a number of female priests and teachers have emerged, many of them married with children. This has changed the way Zen is taught in the West and has seen an emphasis on integrating Zen practice into daily life. Women tend to be less ego-driven and more naturally inclined towards a Zen attitude whilst at the same time having a natural creativity that allows them to develop Zen thought in the Western world. This has brought some Zen women into conflict with their more traditional male teachers and often as not has led to them taking a step away from traditional Zen and creating new paths of teaching and practice. This is not a bad thing as it allows Zen to continue to expand, adjust and develop in the light of forever changing times.

Zen has not only integrated well with Western life, it has also become attractive to many non-Buddhists, especially some Christians. There are Zen-Christian monks and nuns and a growing number of Christian Zen centres. Because Zen is not a religion in the same sense as Christianity, there is no reason why Zazen and Christian belief cannot go hand in hand. Zen also seems to become integrated into the lives of some followers of Judaism and there has even been a rabbi ordained as a Zen priest. We are moving towards a more open dialogue between religions with people focussing more on commonality rather than differences and Zen has much to offer to anyone seeking a deeper understanding of their spiritual path, no matter what their beliefs. Clearly Zen has a role to play in today's changing world.

Thich Nhat Hanh's teachings are simple but profound, such as 'Make the present moment into the most wonderful moment of your life'.

In the West women have played an important role in the development of Zen Buddhism and today there are many highly respected and wise nuns.

Another important trend in Western Buddhism has been its involvement in social problems and issues. There are now Zen chaplains in prisons and Zen Buddhists working with the dying, terminally ill and the homeless or in deprived inner city areas. There are also Buddhists involved with ecology and political activism especially where there is religious intolerance and repression of freedom. Social action is seen by many Zen practitioners as truly following the Buddhist vows of love and compassion for others. Part of this movement has become known as 'Engaged Buddhism' and was developed by Thich Nhat Hanh, a Vietnamese monk from the Thien (Zen) School of Vietnam.

Thich Nhat Hanh was born in 1926 in Vietnam and after a normal education became a Zen monk at the age of 16. With the onset of the Vietnam War he became involved in the All-Vietnamese Buddhist Association, which sought to promote Buddhism as a unifying and pacifying force. In 1961 he was invited to teach Buddhism at Columbia University, America and in 1964 he returned to Vietnam to create the School of Youth for Social Service and the Tipe Hien Order (Order of Interbeing). As well as promoting peace, the order helped in the rebuilding of bombed villages, the creation of clinics and the development of farmers' cooperatives. As a result of his work towards peace he was banished from his home and in 1973, after signing the Peace Accords in Paris, he settled in rural France. From there he continued to support Vietnamese refugees both in France and in the Far East.

His teachings, which extol the virtues of developing a quiet and clear mind, have brought him many followers and his books have sold worldwide and been translated into many languages. He advocates mindfulness of breathing as a simple meditative technique that anyone can do at anytime and anywhere as a means of developing awareness and an open heart to the suffering of the world. In 1969 he was nominated for the Nobel Peace Prize by Martin Luther King, Jr.

ZEN PRINCIPLES

'The Way of the Buddha is to know yourself,
to know yourself is to forget yourself,
to forget yourself is to be enlightened by all things.'

DOGEN

FOUNDATIONS OF ZEN

'The Great Way is always present, but though it is present, it is hard to see.'

PAO-CHIH

The way of Zen is simple, in fact it is so simple that it often eludes people. In the study of Zen your biggest obstacle, your greatest adversary, is your own mind. There are really no other barriers to enlightenment. If you are to succeed in understanding Zen's simple message, all you need to do is master the art of letting go. You need to let go of what you think you know, to stand empty, waiting to be filled with wisdom. How can you learn a new way of thinking unless you first let go of your old ways of thinking? How can you be happy unless you let go of sadness?

Zen is all about living in the here and now. If you are suffering, let go of the root of your suffering and it will cease. So often people let go physically but cannot let go mentally. For instance, if you smoke tobacco and it is causing you to suffer from smoking-related illnesses, stopping smoking will allow your body to heal itself. However, for this to truly work you need not only to stop smoking physically but also to let it go emotionally/mentally. If you still crave a cigarette you have not really let go, you have only pretended to. Your ego has fooled you and so you will still suffer. Letting go means to do so one hundred percent and with pleasure. If you are going to do anything, you might as well do it with pleasure. If you cannot do something with pleasure, then why do it at all?

A Zen proverb very simply states, 'See how we cause ourselves to suffer by resisting what is.' If something has happened, it must have needed to happen and to resist it is not only foolish, but damaging to our very being. Stress is without doubt the biggest cause of ill heath in the Western world and much of that stress comes from our inability to accept things we don't like with pleasure. To have strong preferences is to live in misery. If you really like something, sooner or later you will lose it and not be able to find it again and this will cause you to suffer from loss. Similarly if you really dislike something, sooner or later it will manifest into your life and this will cause you to suffer from resistance. If only we can learn to 'change our minds', to embrace everything with pleasure, to realize that all experience is life enhancing, we would live happy and peaceful lives.

So often we dislike things that are unpleasant or challenging, but it is the challenging times that teach us the most. When life is comfortable we learn very little. A life without mistakes is the life of a fool. Mistakes, challenges, unpleasant situations all incline us to draw on our inner resources and this in turn makes us wiser. Why then dislike the unpleasant? Learn to embrace everything with pleasure and your life will be filled with pleasure. Zen challenges you to change your mind, to think in new, innovative ways, to learn to truly be yourself.

One of the things that often strikes people when they meet a Buddhist monk is their sense of inner wellbeing and joy.

TEN OX-HERDING PICTURES

The ten ox-herding pictures can be found adorning the walls of many Zen monasteries throughout China, Japan and Korea. Originating in Chinese antiquity, these pictures describe the path to enlightenment for a student of Zen, from the moment they enter the Way through to the completion of their training when they become a master in their own right. A series of poems and commentaries is also associated with them to make their message clearer.

1 The Search for the Ox

Tall trees, high mountains, deep waters,
Endlessly I walk in search of the ox.
Tiredness takes hold
Still no ox is found
Just the chirping of locusts in the forest.

This first stage is all about the search. The picture depicts a young man looking rather lost. He is searching for something but is not even clear exactly what it is he is searching for. This stage represents the time prior to embarking on your spiritual quest when you are filled with restlessness and dissatisfaction. This stage often arises when you have sought happiness in things outside of yourself and come back wanting. A good job, financial security, a stable relationship, a nice home, all these things bring only a fleeting sense of inner wellbeing and long-lasting happiness seems as far away and elusive as ever. There must be something more to life, something deeper and more meaningful. All these external things bring their own challenges and still there is no inner peace. Like the young ox herder, the beauty of creation surrounds you yet still you feel empty and lacking. The ox represents the true Self and so the search is for the Self. No wonder it seems so elusive and unobtainable from external things. The dissatisfaction continues like an itch that cannot be scratched, onwards you go, still searching.

2 Finding the Footprints

In mud by the riverbank I find footprints,
In the fragrant grasses I see where he has walked;
In the remote mountain path, there they are again
As plain as the nose on my face.

The second stage represents the first signpost to guide your search. In this picture the ox herder at last discovers footprints and having done so he begins to see them everywhere. How could he have missed them before? There they are in plain view for anyone to see if they have the eyes to see them. This represents the time when having been dissatisfied with life, you decide to do something about it. You begin to ask questions, to read books and hear the first talk about Zen. Something about this path seems to make sense, your curiosity is aroused and the more you read and question, the more inspired you become. The peacefulness of Zen seems almost magical and the stories of finding enlightenment and freedom ring some distant and long-forgotten bell deep within your sub-conscious. You know this path, it now seems familiar and yet how can this be so? Each time you discover a little more about Zen, it raises even more questions in your mind, but something inside of you tells you to keep on searching.

3 Seeing the Ox

The willow sways in the breeze
The nightingale sings on high
In the moon's glow, what can hide?
A glimpse of horns, half hidden in the trees.

Finally the ox herder catches his first glimpse of the ox, although still he does not see it fully. Many Zen teachers consider this stage as a breakthrough stage. It represents the transition from thinking about your spiritual path to actually doing something about it. You might visit a monastery or talk to a Zen teacher; you may continue to read books but for the first time you actually start to try to practise what you have begun to learn about. Finally you try some Zen meditation and the sense of inner peace that you glimpse makes you hunger for ever-deepening experiences. You begin to change the way you act, seeking to integrate some of the Zen precepts into your daily life. A new excitement for living grows within you; you know you've found something even though you are still not exactly sure what you have found. You actually feel different inside, you feel more yourself than you have felt for a very long time. You resolve within your heart to discover more and to not stray from this new path of discovery until you fully understand its true meaning.

4 Catching the Ox

After much struggling I seize him,
His nose is pierced but still he will not pacify;
High and low he drags me
Above the clouds and down into the ravine.

In this picture the ox herder has finally caught the ox and has him roped, but he has to struggle long and hard to keep hold of the rope because the ox does not want to be caught. The ox appears inexhaustible and leads the herder on a merry dance up hill and down dale. It takes all his will power and strength just to keep hold of the beast. This represents your first experience of regular and disciplined practice. The method of meditation appears simple enough, it should be easy to find calmness and peace through just sitting, but this is not the case. The more you try to switch off the mind, the more it chatters away at you during your practice. Not only that, you try to keep the simplest of rules but without success. You know what is right, it even makes sense that it is right but still you find yourself doing the opposite. Here the ox represents the untamed ego, what the Chinese call 'the monkey mind' that will not be quiet and calm. Thoughts of the past and future flood in when you meditate, you feel uncomfortable in the postures, you daydream instead of meditate or worse still you fall asleep. This Zen path is harder than you thought, but something inside makes you determined to carry on.

5 Taming the Ox

Whip and rope are needed
Strength too else he might stray and fall
Heels dug in, the moment passes
Gently now the ox follows his master.

Here the ox herder has tamed the ox. Through struggling and determination he has won through and now the ox is tame. Notice though that the herder does not yet let go of the rope – this is no time for complacency. You continue your practice with determination and slowly but surely it becomes less of a struggle. The postures in meditation are getting less uncomfortable, the mind calms down quicker and you find it easier to just sit and be at one with the breath. Your restlessness has gone and you begin to understand yourself at a deeper level. You know about the natural order of things, you understand how your habits and destructive thought patterns can take you away from that order, you know what makes your fear and anger rise up. 'I've found it' you cry with exhilaration only to realize the next moment that you have lost it. A week later you shout, 'Now I really have found it,' but then it is gone again. Week by week, year by year the revelations continue, each one wiping away the previous one but all the time getting clearer and clearer. 'Where's the end of it?' you ask only to realize that the way is without end.

6 Riding the Ox Home

Mounting the ox, I head homeward.
My flute sings to the setting sun.
No song can tempt me backwards
As we dance to the rhythm of life.

This picture shows that the rope is now gone and the ox herder sits astride the ox happily playing his flute. The ox no longer needs guiding, it knows its own way. Everything is in harmony. This is usually the point of no return for most students as things begin to fall into place. Practice now comes naturally without struggle and the severity of earlier times has been replaced with laughter, joy and lightness. The further you advance, the more you discover about yourself. Hidden talents of creativity rise up and you find yourself drawn towards the Zen arts. It might be poetry, cooking, the art of tea, gardening, music or the martial arts but whatever you turn your hand to is now infused with grace and gentle beauty. Every action becomes an art from the simplest task to the most complex. Life is a thrilling adventure and although you have no real idea what lies around the next corner, excitement has replaced fear and joy has replaced anxiety. For the first time you start to take yourself less seriously and seek only to *go with the flow* understanding that you are part of an ever-changing universe. You finally know what it feels like to be alive.

7 The Ox Transcended

Home at last, I am at peace
The ox can rest too.
At dawn I sit alone in blissful repose,
What need have I of whip and rope?

The ox is gone and the ox herder rests alone. Up to this point you have been on a mission to discover your true Self. You have spent time practising and you have spent time trying to understand. Now practice and understanding have become one. You no longer put time aside to practise because your whole life is now one of living Zen. Your life is a walking meditation and everything you do, you do one hundred percent and with total pleasure. No job is too trivial to demand your complete and undivided attention. Whatever you do, you do fully present to it, and when it is time to move on you let go without regret. You are now at peace with the world, you no longer need to discipline yourself. Following the precepts has become second nature and thoughts of deceit or anger no longer arise. Other students come to you to ask questions or seek guidance and you take on this responsibility with ease. You are preparing to receive the transmission of Dharma from your teacher as you walk with body, mind and spirit in total harmony.

8 Both Ox and Self are Transcended

Whip, rope, ox, self – all are transcended
What obstacles remain?
Can a snowflake shine in a raging fire?
With laughter I walk with the ancestors.

The ox and ox herder are both gone. All that remains is a black circle, which represents emptiness. Up until now you have had the sense that 'I am practising' the notions of 'me' and 'mine'. Now you realize that you own nothing. You realize that you are no more than a caretaker of things that come and go. You experience the feelings of having no solid, separate identity. You are an amalgamation of ancestral DNA, social conditioning, national identity, dietary choices etc. You no longer hold on to feelings, thoughts and possessions. They come and they go. Everything is transitory. You hold on to nothing and have nowhere to go. The liberation this brings is a whole new experience. You feel light, hollow, transparent; empty and yet full. You hold in each moment an infinity of possibilities, of endless transformations. There is no more grasping, no struggle, just your buddhanature shining through. It is at this point that the process of transmission from master to student truly begins. It will continue in the next picture and reach completion in the final picture. This stage is not true enlightenment, but more of a glimpse of it; the beginnings of an opening through which the student will step.

9 Return to the Source

After much vainless effort, I return to the source;
Better I were blind, deaf and dumb from the
*   beginning.*
The mountains and river are just so,
The flowers bright and fragrant.

This picture depicts creation in all its beauty and fullness. What was empty has now become full; yin has turned to yang. If you stay with emptiness, you risk isolation and separation; so it is only right that you return to the world reborn as your true Self. All things now enlighten you. A simple meal takes on deep meaning as you connect with the spirit of the grains and vegetables, the earth, sun and rain and the love of the person who prepared it for you. Your life is now unremarkable but with a depth that cannot be explained. All your thoughts, words and actions are at one with the world. After all this practice and hard discipline, you find that the truth you were seeking was right in front of you all the time. At this point of training, the paths of monk and layperson diverge. Monks will begin learning tantric teachings and other trainings in preparation for performing liturgy (service) and ceremonies, for ordaining monks and in readiness for their role as temple priest or monastery abbot. The layperson trains in readiness to work with lay students on self-realization, zazen and koan study. They may, like monks, perform daily liturgies but will work from a training centre with people who have jobs, families and hobbies etc.

10 Into the World

Barefooted and in rags
I walk among the people of the world.
Even covered in dust, I remain in bliss;
As a child I look in wonder
At the flowers blooming on the withered tree.

This picture shows a ragged, pot-bellied man walking barefoot and carrying a sack filled with gifts. This is the final stage of the path to enlightenment. Now you understand how to walk with freedom, wisdom and compassion. You are no longer worried about appearances and can adapt freely to any and all possible situations. You are at home with the highest royalty and the poorest peasant. Your bag is filled with the gifts of love, compassion, understanding, joy, laughter and wisdom that you dispense freely and endlessly to all who are willing to receive. You give, seeking nothing in return and remain always humble. You find spirituality in everything and everyone and love all creation without condition. Even the withered, dying tree has beauty in your eyes, likewise the sad, grumpy, angry and hurt people of the world whom you meet on your path. You embrace everything with pleasure, seeking only to bring lightness into the lives of others. You listen intently, observe quietly and respond appropriately without forcing your ideas or opinions on others. You are full of grace and beauty. You are truly yourself.

When considering the ten ox-herding pictures, it would be a mistake to think that the path to enlightenment is a straight line. You will visit each of these stages many times on your path. Once you reach any stage, often you return to earlier stages to understand them at a deeper and more profound level. Enlightenment is an on-going process and you can have many awakenings during a lifetime. There is no end just as there is no beginning. The tenth picture is not so different from the first picture – the beginner's mind. Openness, naiveté, innocence are as much the qualities of the master as the beginner. All is one. The Way unfolds endlessly covering the whole universe, and though its mesh is wide it lets nothing slip through.

THE THREE ATTITUDES

The Three Attitudes developed through the practice of Zen are Great Faith, Great Doubt and Great Courage. The great Zen masters have all expounded on these fundamental qualities. Though these qualities are simple enough to understand, it is far more challenging to put them to use in daily life. The Three Attitudes are not a goal. Rather, they are an ongoing and forever deepening experience of living Zen. Paradoxically, to think you have achieved them is to lose sight of them altogether!

Great Faith

Great Faith is a belief in your ability to realize your 'buddhanature', your innate potential to be enlightened and the understanding that if you follow a Zen path, you are inevitably walking towards enlightenment. It is this faith that helps you continue on the path, especially when you feel as if you are making no progress whatsoever.

Faith in others is of no use in Zen practice, for it distracts you from faith in your Self. This principle is demonstrated in the Zen saying, 'If you see the Buddha walking down the road, kill him!' This startling statement means that if you perceive someone else as fully enlightened, it is an indication that you have lost the Great Faith in your own potential for enlightenment and are projecting it instead onto another person. 'Kill him!' means 'end your illusionary, external thinking and return to your inner faith'.

Faith, however, is not simply belief. It is something much deeper. You may have been drawn to Zen for a great many reasons. You might feel an inner calling; you might meet it through a friend, a book, a lecture. At first you practise because you believe Zen is leading you into a deeper understanding of yourself. However, when the going gets tough, as it inevitably must to challenge your strongly held beliefs, it is faith that gets you through. Truth requires no belief; it is just the truth. It follows that to hold strong beliefs is

to hold 'un-truths'. The truth requires no proof; nor does it need defending. It stands firmly on its own.

Similarly, Great Faith is a deep inner knowing that cannot be challenged nor weakened by anything life might throw at you. It is the power that carries you through the darkest times. Faith comes with practice. The more you practise, the more positive change you can see in yourself and the greater your faith becomes to sustain you on your path.

Great Doubt

It may appear contradictory to hold the attitude of Great Faith and Great Doubt together, but without Great Doubt we learn nothing. As the Zen saying tells:

Great Doubt, Great Awakening;
Little Doubt, Little Awakening;
No Doubt, No Awakening.

Great Doubt is the inspiration that keeps you walking a path of learning. Once you think you know and understand something, there is no longer any point in studying it. To be forever questioning is to be forever learning. How many couples think they know their partner and are devastated when that partner does the unexpected? To think you know is folly. The greatest peace of mind lies in not knowing. Once you realize that you do not really know anything, every experience in life is a new adventure of deepening understanding. A couple who realize that they do not really know each other, are forever making fresh discoveries about one another, therefore their relationship remains fresh and new, even after many years. It is the same with the Zen path; this is the power of Great Doubt.

Great Courage

It takes Great Courage to follow the Zen path because you are forever walking into the unknown. One needs courage to live in the present, for to do so means letting go of the past and the future. The courage to admit the folly of how you have run your life and the mistakes you have made, to truly face up to your inner Self, to refuse to be moved by the judgment or ridicule of others, all these take true courage. Conversely, it takes little courage to fight with someone else, especially as most people enter a fight with the belief that they will win. It takes much more courage to fight your own ego, to look at yourself with true honesty. This honest and courageous introspection born of Great Courage is the foundation of Zen practice.

KARMA .

Karma is perhaps one of the most misunderstood concepts of Buddhism. It is often referred to as the law of cause and effect and means that every action of mind, body or spirit creates a cause that will at some point in the future have an effect. This effect can even come in a future rebirth as karma keeps us locked in *samsara* (the cycle of birth, death and rebirth). Karma is basically the result of our own lack of spiritual awareness and the illusion we hold that we are individual, independent entities. We think of Self over and above everyone else and our attachment to desire is the root cause of our karma.

Human beings have two fundamental driving forces, the desire to eat and the desire to sexually reproduce. These basic instincts are born out of a desire for self-preservation and so have a very powerful effect on our lives. We find it difficult to control our sexual desire and the world is rife with sexual scandals and love affairs. Likewise our appetite for food is so strong that obesity is now a worldwide epidemic. Humans eat everything without thought and in the West the desire for cheap food means that both human and animal welfare are continually compromised so that we can satisfy our endless desires. Every time you eat meat you create karma, every time you buy cheap food you create karma. Factory farming cares nothing for the suffering of others be they animal or human. Just because you don't kill the animal yourself or pay the ridiculously low wages of foreign factory workers does not mean that you escape the karmic consequences of eating meat. Ignorance is no excuse!

Attachment to emotion and thought are the other factors that tend to create karma for an individual. We all experience emotion and our emotions fall into two categories, transient and sustained. If your life is threatened by danger, for example, you feel a mixture of fear, shock and anger. However, once the danger is passed you feel relief and joy. These are transient emotions and tend to have less karmic ramifications. Sustained emotions are much more potentially damaging and arise as a result of upbringing, social conditioning and morality. It is when we become fixated on these emotions, whether good or bad, that we create karma. The most problematic of emotions are the passionate ones such as fear, hatred, anger and joy. If we become fixated on any of these emotions they become embedded deep in our subconscious and continually influence how we run our lives. Racism, phobias, prejudice, addictions and strong preferences all have the potential to create deep karma because they have the power to block

*'As long as you are subject to a life bound by force of habit,
you are not free from the burden of the body.'*

KUEI-SHAN OF THE HOUSE OF TSAO-TING

out reason. Often these deep-seated emotions can be carried on from generation to generation causing endless suffering on many levels. Karma is not created by emotions and ideas themselves, only by our attachment to them.

We accrue positive or negative karma through our actions of body, speech and mind, the intent behind those actions and the results of those actions. Actions that are selfish or self-centred accrue negative karma and actions that are self-less and centred on unconditional love accrue positive karma. This might sound simple and it is, although our understanding of selfish and selfless can be distorted by our emotional attachments. A wife who selflessly pleases her husband because of fear or guilt is not accruing positive karma. If you compromise your own happiness in order to make your children happy all you are doing is teaching them by your example that they should compromise their own happiness for others. This might appear selfless but in fact it just perpetuates the cycle of suffering from one generation to the next.

What you sow is what you reap and all your actions have consequences for you at some point in the future. If you live a life filled with selfish desires and you use fear and intimidation to gain success, you will pay a price for that in this life or the next. Where people misunderstand karma is when challenges occur in their own lives. Having a difficult and challenging life does not necessarily mean that you were a 'bad' person in a previous life. Often we only perceive challenges as bad because of our own preferences. A challenging life may actually be the result of the accumulation of positive karma because challenges make us look deeper within ourselves and connect us with inner resources.

Actions that are not centred around Self, but are born out of unconditional love, create positive karma and a mutual sense of inner wellbeing.

THE THREE TRAININGS

For any student of Zen to make spiritual progress it is essential that they study and learn the three trainings of ethics, meditation and wisdom. These form the foundation of Zen practice. All three trainings need to be studied in unison for them to have any real power in our lives. Ethics, when practised alone, can tend to make us narrow-minded and judgemental. Meditation, when practised without the other two trainings, can lead us into being self-absorbed and withdrawn from the world. Wisdom, when practised alone can make us appear analytical and superior. Only by practising all three together can we hope to achieve balance and make progress on our spiritual path.

Ethics

Ethics or morality can be divided into two areas; firstly how we run our lives and secondly our relationship with the world around us. How we run our lives is about taking full responsibility for our thoughts and conduct. Buddha taught that there are five hindrances which slow down progress on our spiritual path. These are sensual desire, ill will, sloth, worry and confused doubt.

Sensual desire relates to the five senses and can include obsession with food, drugs or sex. Following these desires brings only short-term happiness followed by a feeling of dissatisfaction as the happiness fades. Sensual desires keep us fixed on a treadmill seeking endless satisfaction through external stimuli and take us on a journey towards further suffering and misery.

Ill will is born out of personal hatred. When you truly love your Self you will have no ill will towards anyone. What you see in others is a direct reflection of what is within you; so if you think ill of someone else you also feel the same way about you. The best way to counteract ill will is to consciously send love and goodwill towards those people you dislike.

Eating a balanced, healthy diet and taking regular gentle exercise best counteracts sloth. Over-eating makes the mind and body sluggish. Walking, Tai Chi and yoga are all forms of exercise that help harmonize mind and body.

Worry often arises when we are over-attached to something or someone, or when we have a guilty conscience. Both are resolved through letting go and having the inner resolve to change the way we think. Meditation can be very helpful in alleviating this problem.

'Realization without making sure of right and wrong is of dubious benefit.'

GUON

Confused doubt comes through thinking too much and filling the mind with endless questions. It is perfectly correct to ask questions, but once a question is asked, it is best to let the answer find you. The more you practise Zen and study its teachings, the less confusion you will have.

Our relationship with the world around us is connected to our interaction with people, creatures and things and how our behaviour affects us and the world at large. Buddha taught five basic precepts that guard against us causing suffering in the world; these are: do not kill, do not take that which is not given, do not misuse the senses, do not lie and do not misuse intoxicants.

These precepts are linked to the five hindrances and none of these negative behaviours will arise if we have mastered these hindrances. Cultivation of these precepts should occur not only in the body through right action but also in the mind and speech. How often have we said, 'I'll kill him' when angry with a friend or how often have we had inappropriate sexual fantasies that would be damaging and destructive if carried out? To live ethically means to embody morals in thought, word and deed. The five precepts are not hard and fast rules that must always be obeyed no matter what. There are times to apply them but also times to let them go. The common example given for this in Zen training is if you are walking in a forest and a deer runs in front of you and off to the left, then a hunter appears and asks you which way the deer went, you might decide to tell a lie and say that the deer ran off to the right. The important thing to remember is that we follow ethics in order to live lives with greater awareness and compassion.

Meditation

Meditation is a process that cultivates concentration and enquiry. Concentration stills the mind, calming down its usual chatter and allows clarity to arise. This clarity then allows us to enquire in a constructive way. Meditation creates a situation where the answers to

our questions come and find us. In the west we tend to fill our minds with so many questions and judgements that there is never any room for the answer to be heard. Next time you have a burning question about your life, try asking it and then forgetting it, putting it out of your mind. Then wait for the answer to come and find you.

At some point in your life you will most likely come across a problem that no matter how hard you try to think about it the answer eludes you. Eventually frustration forces you to let go of the problem and do something else instead. As you engage in other activities you begin to forget the problem. Then, when you least expect it and when you aren't even thinking about it, up pops the answer into your mind. What has happened is that the subconscious mind has taken over thinking and processing the problem. It has searched its many databanks until it found the answer. Then it waited for the opportunity to let that answer rise up into the conscious mind. It usually uses a time when you are doing something so mundane that you don't have to think about it, you just do it *without thinking*. That's the trick of meditation. It is so mundane that you end up doing it without thinking and if you do it every day, it means that every day your subconscious mind can talk to you and help you better navigate the challenges of life.

Many people believe that we have a 'higher Self', a part of us that understands everything: why we are here, what lessons we have to learn this time around and what choices are best to facilitate that learning. It speaks to us through the subconscious; through dreams, intuitions and meditation. Unlike our ego, it does not force itself upon us. It waits patiently and speaks quietly, like our own inner Zen master. We may not fully understand what it is saying, we might even become more confused for a while by listening

to it, but if we are patient it will guide us towards all the answers we are looking for. Meditation, when practised at its highest level, is sitting with your own, personal Zen master.

Wisdom

Zen wisdom basically knows to eat rice from a bowl, that it is a bowl and not a cattle trough, and how to be fully in the present experiencing the moment, the taste of the rice, its colour, its aroma, its feel in your mouth yet without taking hold of the rice or the bowl or ourselves or anything else. Zen wisdom cannot be learned from books or from studying with many Zen masters. It arises naturally from within us the moment we choose to fully let go. We let go of the pain of the past, the dreams and fantasies of the future and become enthused by each and every passing moment.

How often do we live in regret, wishing we had done something that we did not or said something when we kept silent? Often we say 'If only I had known then what I know now, I would have acted differently'. One of the hardest things some people have to come to terms with is the unexpected death of a loved one. What makes it particularly difficult is when the last things they shared were harsh words or anger. They live with permanent regret tinged with guilt for how they acted. What they wish they had said was 'I love you' but instead of sharing love they shared pain. When you learn to fully let go of the past, you begin to live a life totally free of guilt and regret. You understand that the past is just a memory, the future just a dream and here and now is all that matters. You become fully present in the moment taking hold of nothing and letting nothing go. This is Zen wisdom.

If you see a deer in a forest and a hunter comes and asks you which way it went, telling him a lie may be the best course of action.

MINDFULNESS

Mindfulness is the key to inner calm. It means being fully present in the here and now and yet not attached to anything. It is not about becoming detached, but being unattached yet fully aware and interested in the unfolding of every moment. Mindfulness is perhaps the most important and relevant of all Zen practices to those living in the Western world.

We live in a world that is filled with images and sensations designed to take hold of our minds. Advertisers seek to tell us how to think, what to like and what to dislike. Fashion tells us how to dress and look and education tells us how to think. Most people are unaware of just how much they are influenced by the outside world. We also tend to 'lose our minds' by becoming involved in the dramas that manifest into our lives. We get lost in thoughts of the past such as regret or nostalgia, in thoughts of the future such as daydreaming and fantasy and in the emotions such thoughts evoke.

The Four Foundations of Mindfulness

In the Zen tradition there are four foundations of mindfulness: mindfulness of the body, of feeling, of thinking and of the objects of thought.

Mindfulness of the Body

When we become mindful of the body, we embark on an adventure of self-discovery. The human body is the most wonderful creation. It takes in air and food and converts them into pure energy. It moves so that we can experience different environments and situations. When sick or injured it heals itself, when tired it rests. By being mindful of the body we can take an active part in achieving inner balance and harmony making us more able to adapt to the constant changes that life brings.

Mindfulness of Feeling

This is about noticing our feelings but not getting lost in them. So often our minds become 'possessed' by feelings. We feel powerless to stop unpleasant feelings or become addicted to seeking out pleasurable feelings. Mindfulness of feeling is about feeling the feeling but not believing it. Have you ever stubbed your toe? It is without doubt a very painful experience. When this happens, most people are

When we are mindful of the body and of feeling, we can learn to appreciate the beauty of every moment.

'There is no Buddha outside your own heart.'

BUNAN

shocked by the pain, then anger arises as they dance around the room cursing the inanimate object they stubbed. The mindful approach to this is to observe the pain, to note where it starts and where it ends. In this way we begin to put our pain into perspective. This observation immediately lessens our perception of pain. The mindful person takes full responsibility for how they are feeling. They are neither angry with themselves nor with the object they struck with their foot. They take full responsibility for stubbing their toe and realize that the pain is nothing more than the body clearly communicating when it is injured. Finally the mindful person is aware of the fact that there is a lesson in everything and so learns from the experience and thus avoids doing it again. In this way we develop a natural ability to avoid accidents and mishaps.

In Zen mistakes are regarded as stepping stones across the river of life to a deeper understanding of Self.

'A cup of tea has no thoughts… it tastes the same to Buddhists as it does to Christians. There is not the slightest difference there.'

KOUN YAMADA

Mindfulness of Thought

This forms the basis of Zen meditation. Zen teaches that all life should be a walking meditation, so mindfulness of thought is a constant goal, not just a practice that takes place during meditation. By observing our thoughts as if from a distance, we find it much easier to let them go. If we are worried about something, concentrating on how our thoughts have caused us to worry rather than becoming overtaken with those thoughts is part of practising mindfulness. If you find yourself in a fearful situation, rather than being lost in the fear or overtaken by it, try observing it with interest. You will then notice how your body reacts to it: your breathing becomes shallow, your shoulders tense and your stomach tightens. By doing this you will lessen your perception of fear. You might then consciously try to breathe a bit deeper and relax your shoulders. This will further reduce your level of anxiety. This will help you to let go of the fear and return to a place of balance and harmony.

Mindfulness of the Objects of Thought

This is the key to letting destructive and pointless thoughts go. Blame is an emotion we use to relinquish our personal responsibility. We blame others for how we feel, or the weather, or the car that won't start or any other object that comes to mind. The truth is we are always totally and fully responsible for how we feel because we choose how to react to any situation. If someone is nasty towards you, you have a choice as to whether you become upset by that behaviour or not. If you take it personally as an attack you will undoubtedly become lost in emotions of blame, anger and sadness. If you are mindful you will perhaps see that the person is actually expressing their own pain and upset. This will then make you more compassionate towards them rather than angry and defensive. By being mindful of the objects of our blame, we break the illusion that we are victims and so do not become lost in emotion.

Practising Mindfulness

1 Mindfulness of the body: Start to become more aware of the functioning of your body. Perhaps the best way to do this is to observe your breathing and eating. Start to notice your breathing pattern and how it changes with your changing environment. Take note also of how you eat. Do you prepare your food with love or just grab the nearest edible object whenever you are hungry? When eating a meal, experience the taste of each individual component of that meal. Observe how you chew and how you breathe while eating.

2 Mindfulness of feeling: Observe how you feel throughout the day. Do you get anxious at certain times? Do you wake up filled with joy for life or dread for the day ahead? How often do you feel angry, sad, tired or hungry? This can be a life-changing experience as you begin to see just how ruled by emotions and feelings you are.

3 Mindfulness of thought: If you begin to see your thoughts arise and then pass, you will realize that they are not actually an integral part of your being. This will then give you

the power to change them. Mindfulness of thought takes practice, and the more you practise the deeper your awareness becomes. Daily zazen practice first thing in the morning is one of the best ways to set you up to practise mindfulness of thought throughout the rest of the day.

4 Mindfulness of the objects of thought: Labelling our thoughts and feelings can help to lessen their impact on our lives. By noticing we feel fear or anger, we already lessen that feeling. This in turn leads to more peacefulness of body, mind and spirit.

HOLDING ON TO NOTHING, LETTING NOTHING GO

The Zen idea of 'holding on to nothing, letting nothing go' is all about not exerting your will on the world but remaining true to your Self. People often hold on to things for fear that if they let them go they will lose them forever. They hold on to possessions, lovers, children and sentimental memories as well as anger, resentment, blame and judgments. They also let things go that they feel are no longer appropriate in their lives such as childishness, bad memories and intuition.

The truth is that we need hold on to nothing for we have the whole universe at our fingertips. To understand this better find a small pebble and imagine that it represents something precious to you. Take hold of the pebble in your hand and turn your hand so that the palm is facing downwards. Now let go of the pebble and notice what happens to the stone. Hopefully, if gravity is working, you will have seen the pebble fall to the floor. Take hold of the pebble once again but this time turn your hand so that the palm is facing upwards. Now let go of the stone. It should still be sitting in the palm of your

open hand. You have let go of it yet it still remains with you.

If we take hold of things, we lose sight of their value and they become nothing more than a burden to us. If, however, we hold everything in the open palm of our hands, things can come and go as they need to without us exerting our will upon them. Take, for example, childhood. It is one of the most exciting and adventurous times of life. When people reach adulthood they either take hold of their childhood memories and get lost in sentimentality or they reject childhood altogether as being no longer appropriate

If you hold all experience in the open palm of your hand, you have the key to happiness, health and freedom.

in their lives. Those who hold on to their childhood tend to act childishly at inappropriate times especially when emotionally upset, and those who reject their childhood forget how to use the imagination and have fun. But why not let childhood just be? In this way it can come to you at appropriate times and fade into the background when it is not needed. There is a time to be purely childish, for instance when playing with children. There is also a time to be purely adult, for instance when a crisis or accident has occurred. If we hold on to or reject childishness, we lose the ability to adapt to changing situations.

Holding on to negative emotions such as fear causes us a great deal of suffering. By metaphorically allowing our emotions to sit in the open palm of our hands, they can come and go as they need to. Most

Even trials and tribulations can become deep adventures of learning if you walk into every experience with open arms.

of the time fear is an inappropriate emotion that when held on to can be very destructive. But if we let this emotion go we lose our ability to protect ourselves. When standing in the road with a lorry heading towards you at speed, it is fear that makes you move out of the way. This is appropriate fear. If, however, you hold on to fear, it may be that fear will take hold of you and instead of moving out of the way of the lorry, you stand there unable to move for the fear and get knocked down. There is a time to be fearful and a time to let fear go.

Is That So? A Zen Story

There was once a Chinese town where a blacksmith lived with his wife and 16-year-old daughter. Just outside the town on a nearby hillside, there was a Zen monastery. The blacksmith was a very strict father who believed in traditional values such as honesty and marriage. One day his daughter, who was secretly seeing a farmer's son, realized she was pregnant. She was filled with fear because she knew her father would be very angry, so she decided to try to keep her pregnancy a secret. However by the sixth month it became obvious that she was pregnant and when her father realized this he demanded of her who the father was? Fearing for the safety of the young man she loved, she decided to tell a lie. 'It was the abbot of the monastery who got me pregnant,' she told her father. At this the father stormed out of the house and went to the monastery to confront the abbot.

As he arrived at the monastery, the abbot was leading the monks in a ceremony. Disregarding what was going on, the father raced up to the abbot and pulling him to his feet said, 'You got my daughter pregnant. You are the father, therefore you must take care of the child when it is born. It is your responsibility,' to which the abbot replied, 'Is that so?' With this the father went home. Three months later the child was born, a baby girl, and after a week the father kept his word and took the child back to the monastery. This time the abbot was meditating. Again the father pulled the abbot to his feet and handing him the baby said, 'You are the father of this child. She is your responsibility and you will take care of her,' to which the abbot replied, 'Is that so?'

As the days passed the blacksmith's daughter missed her baby more and more. After two weeks she could bear it no longer and so she went to her father and told him the truth. She told him that she had lied about the abbot being the father and that it was the farmer's son who was really the father. She told him of their love and how they wanted to marry and

When the blacksmith first confronted the abbot and accused him of fathering the child of a girl he did not know, the abbot could have reacted in all sorts of ways. He could have immediately defended himself, either by vehemently denying it or by becoming angry at the rudeness of the interruption of a sacred ceremony. He could have told the blacksmith how it was impossible for him to take care of a child. He was an abbot with no experience of parenthood; besides what would all his monks think? Instead the abbot simply accepted. He did not take hold of any emotion nor did he let go of his inner calm. If you do not allow yourself to be moved by the emotions of others, you are free to embrace everything that comes into your life.

bring the child up themselves. The father was very angry, especially as he had accused an innocent man of a wrong he did not commit. Immediately he went up to the monastery and on entering found the abbot in the garden feeding the baby some goat's milk. He walked straight up to the abbot, took the baby from him and said, 'You are not the father of this child, it is not your responsibility to take care of her,' to which the abbot replied, 'Is that so?'

The Perhaps Way: A Zen Story

In a small farming village long ago there lived a widowed farmer with his son. The farmer was very poor owning only one horse and a small piece of farmland that he and his son worked on to support themselves. They lived a simple but happy life and every morning the farmer rose at dawn and stepped from his lowly dwelling outside to greet the rising sun. He would stand, bathing in the sun's rays and thank creation for its wonder and beauty.

One morning he arose as usual and performed his morning ritual, then roused his son and the two shared a simple breakfast together. He then went to feed his horse. When he arrived at his paddock, he found several men of the village gathered around its gate, which was broken. There was no sign of his horse. 'Oh you poor man,' they cried, 'your only horse has bolted and run off into the wilderness. How now will you plough your fields? The gods must be very angry with you; you must have done something bad to have invoked their fury in this way,' to which the farmer replied, 'Perhaps'.

The next morning the farmer arose as usual and after breakfast went to his paddock to repair the broken gate. As he arrived he once again found the same group of men by his paddock. There was the farmer's horse and six wild horses standing in the paddock. 'You are the luckiest man alive,' they cried. 'Your horse has returned and brought six others with it. You are rich beyond your dreams. The gods are smiling on you this day,' to which the farmer replied, 'Perhaps'.

The next morning the farmer's son arose and decided break in one of the horses. He climbed on its back but he was soon thrown off and as he hit the ground he broke his leg. The villagers said to the farmer, 'you poor man. Your only help cannot work for the next six weeks. You will have to tend your crops alone. You are the unluckiest man alive,' to which the farmer said, 'Perhaps.'

The next morning before dawn, the farmer was awoken by a great commotion. He stepped

This story clearly illustrates the folly of making judgments. We never really know whether something that occurs is good or bad. Often what appears to be the worst thing turns out to be the best thing. Similarly what appears good can sometimes turn out to be bad. Just because life appears uncomfortable does not necessarily mean that you should feel bad about it. If we can embrace all circumstances with pleasure, rather than judgments, difficult times pass more quickly and we learn to make the best of every situation we find ourselves in. The next time you feel like you are having bad luck, remember the perhaps way and embrace your bad luck by being present in each and every moment.

outside his home to find many soldiers in the village. One of the village men came to him saying, 'we are all doomed. The emperor is at war with a rival and all young men who are fit and able are being taken from us to fight. You are so lucky that your son has a broken leg. He will soon heal but many of our sons will never come back. The gods must like you,' to which the farmer replied, 'Perhaps.'

NO-MIND, ONE-MIND, CLEAR-MIND

Zen teaches about three states of mind; no-mind, one-mind and clear mind. To understand these we can look at how different mind states react to the same extraordinary situation. This situation involves a couple who are in their home one evening when an armed robber breaks in and confronts them, demanding money.

The couple in a no-mind state might be making love when the robber arrives. They are lost in mutual ecstasy, their senses bombarded with waves of pleasure. Imagine their shock and horror as the robber shouts at them 'Give me your money!' They will, in just a few seconds, find themselves catapulted from heaven into hell. Filled with shock and fear they hand over their money and the robber leaves. Soon their shock turns to anger and regret and their fear becomes their daily reality.

You meet this couple two years later and they still talk about 'the night that ruined our lives'. They tell the story of that night with the robber, how they wish they had never moved to that area, how they cannot sleep at night for fear of intruders, how they cannot make love anymore because it reminds them of that terrible night, how they felt so defiled and so on. Endless pain, torment and suffering is all they talk about. 'But you survived,' you might say, 'why hang on to the past? Why not celebrate the fact that you are still alive?' They both look at you in utter amazement as if you were insane and say together, 'But you don't understand, I can still feel the gun against my head.'

This is no-mind. People who live like this do not need to wonder whether they will go to heaven or hell when they die because they are already living in hell. The past is just a memory and we have a choice whether we hold on to the pain of the past or let it go. But those people who live all their lives in a no-mind state seeking endless sensorial pleasure find it very hard to see it that way.

The one-mind couple in our story are meditating when the armed robber bursts in. They are lay-Buddhists and are actively seeking enlightenment. Their teacher told them to meditate for two hours every morning and evening between the hours of eight and ten reciting the mantra, 'Om mani padme on'. It is unfortunate that the robber arrives at nine o'clock demanding money because all the couple do is to sit cross-legged saying, 'Om mani padme on'. 'Don't you realize that I will kill you if you don't give me the money,' shouts the robber. But the couple understand that death is life and life is death, all is one, everything is 'Om mani padme on'. Filled with rage the robber shoots both of them in the head and then steals their money. The moral of this story is that one-mindedness is not the middle way. It is an extreme and has the potential to do you great harm.

The clear-mind couple in our story are making love when the robber bursts in and demands money. Showing no fear at all they ask him how much of their money he wants. 'All of it,' comes the reply. So they collect together all of their money, every last bit, and give it to the robber. He leaves and they might even go back to making love again, giving the incident no more thought. This couple are truly enlightened.

Meditation is very useful for helping to clear the mind, but if we become obsessed with meditation, we become one-minded and lose sight of our goal.

THE ART OF ACCEPTANCE

One of the most potentially life-changing skills of Zen Buddhism is the Art of Acceptance. It is a skill that, when mastered, changes the whole colour of life. For many ordinary people, life is a cycle of light and dark. They have light, happy times in their lives that are filled with life-enhancing experiences such as falling in love, the birth of a child and achieving a goal. They also have dark, unhappy times in their lives that are filled with pain and suffering such as arguing or breaking up with a partner, the death of a loved one and failure. Imagine what life would be like if the dark times no longer existed. How wonderful life would be if every moment were filled with light and life-enhancing experiences. Such a life is not a fantasy; it is a moment-by-moment reality for those who have learned the Art of Acceptance.

Acceptance means to favourably receive, to embrace without judgment. Zen teaches us that suffering only comes when we cannot accept what is. It is not what has occurred that causes us to suffer, but our resistance to accept it. Life is filled with lessons and it is acceptance that shows us how to learn those lessons by finding the positive in everything. Even what appears to be the darkest of times has an equal and opposite amount of light in it for those who can open their eyes to see it. So often we are so busy resisting what has happened that we fail to see the light. It is our judgments and desires that block our path to acceptance. If we desire only experiences in our lives that give pleasure to our senses, we are doomed to a life of misery. When we judge things as 'bad', we subconsciously punish ourselves for allowing bad things to happen to us. Most people have some sense of karma and subconsciously think that if something 'bad' happens to you it must be some kind of divine punishment for a wrong you have done in the past. However, if you take away the perception of things being 'bad', then you live beyond karma in *heaven on earth*.

Everything happens for a reason and acceptance allows us the freedom to be able to understand those reasons. It is nothing more or less than a 'change of mind'. It is about choosing to embrace everything with pleasure and to actively seek to find the positive in everything. Let us take some examples of things that make us suffer so we can understand the art of acceptance at a deeper level. Arguments, especially in relationships, are a cause of great suffering in the world today. When someone argues, what they are actually doing is trying to impose their view on

If we learn the art of acceptance, every moment is filled with wonder and takes us deeper into happiness, health and freedom.

another person. 'I am right and you are wrong,' is the initial communication in an argument. Next time you feel yourself about to be drawn into an argument, ask yourself the question, 'Do I want to be free to think what I want and how I want?' If the answer is 'Yes!' then you have to allow all those around you the freedom to think what and how they want. The laws of karma show that if you seek to imprison others, you will yourself become imprisoned. If you seek to dictate to others how they should think, you will lose your own freedom to think for your Self. Don't argue; just accept that other people have the right to be free to think what they like, even if it is the exact opposite of what you think.

When a relationship between two lovers breaks up, the requirement for acceptance is deeper, especially if a third party is involved. Imagine the person you love leaves you a note one day saying that they have left you for your best friend. How would you react? If you cannot accept, you will have feelings of anger, betrayal and deceit. How could they do this to me? How cowardly to leave me a note and not speak to me face to face. How long has this been going on? How dare they treat me in this way? All these questions arise from desire. But consider some other questions. If you love your partner and your best friend, don't you want them to be happy above all else? If they would be happier with each other should not your love for them be strong and deep enough to let them go? Perhaps your partner wrote to you rather than speaking face to face because of guilt and fear. Should you not feel compassion for someone you love who is carrying such emotions? The only pure, lasting love is unconditional love and acceptance is the price we pay for it. For most people love is conditional and so quickly turns to hate if situations such as the one described above manifests into their lives.

The death of a loved one requires an even deeper level of acceptance. To accept the death of a loved

'When wisdom arises it dispels the darkness of ignorance, creates the illumination of knowledge, shines the light of understanding and makes holy truths stand out clearly.'

BUDDHA

one is to honour their life. When someone we love dies, it is perfectly natural to feel grief. Grief is an important adjustment process to a major change occurring in our lives. But it does not have to be a time of suffering. Death can be as life-giving as birth. When we accept death, we open our minds to all the lessons that a life shared has taught us. Many times loved ones have inspired us in our lives teaching us by their example. They sometimes teach us how to be and at other times teach us how not to be. The times we shared with them were full of many lessons and by learning those lessons we honour the lives of loved ones even after their passing. This then allows us to be in a place of love rather than a place of sorrow and love is the one thing that is not bound by life or death.

Finally acceptance of failure is acceptance of wisdom. The person who does not fail does not learn. Failure is nothing more than a lesson waiting to be learned. All the successful people in the world became successful through failure. Failure is not getting something wrong; it is an important aspect of achieving success. There is a famous saying, 'If at first you don't succeed, try, try again'. But to try is to invite failure. If someone says to you, 'I tried to get up early this morning,' what they are telling you is that they failed to get up early. A Zen version of this saying might say, 'If at first you don't succeed, do, do again.' Just do what you do and if the outcome is not what you expected, accept it and learn from it. Then do it again using your new understanding to modulate your actions. If you are not attached to outcomes, there is no such thing as failure, only lessons. Do away with success and failure, accept everything that happens as needing to happen, and wisdom and happiness will be yours.

Buddhist funerals are ceremonies to honour a life, rather than mourn a death.

THE WAY OF THE BODHISATTVA

One of the central teachings of Mahayana Buddhism that has continued in the Zen tradition is the bodhisattva ideal. A bodhisattva is an individual who has experienced an awakening and who dedicates his or her life to helping others achieve the same. In early Buddhism, once an individual achieved enlightenment they entered nirvana, which means the cessation of individual existence. This meant that they were free from the endless round of birth, death and rebirth (samsara). The bodhisattva, however, chooses to remain in samsara until all sentient beings are enlightened.

A bodhisattva begins his or her journey by awakening the 'mind of enlightenment'. This can be seen as gaining an initial insight into our true buddhanature. This insight might last but a few moments but is so profound that the bodhisattva vows to diligently practise until enlightenment becomes a continual reality. They do this not for selfish reasons but for the sake of all beings. In the Zen tradition this commitment is expressed as the Four Great Vows:

Sentient beings are numberless; I vow to save them.
Delusions are inexhaustible; I vow to end them.
The Dharma Gates are boundless; I vow to
   master them.
The Buddha's way is unsurpassable; I vow to attain it.

For a bodhisattva the vow to save all beings is born out of compassion and a selfless intent. How can we achieve this in our daily lives? Often when we think about saving others from suffering we think of the Third World and how we can help the poor by giving them food, education and healthcare. But for a bodhisattva it is the people he or she meets day by day who are the focus of their intent. In the West there is relative affluence and it is often not physical suffering that most people need saving from but mental suffering. This suffering comes from duality and makes people feel isolated and alone even when surrounded by others. People tend to build walls around themselves in an attempt to protect them but this only compounds the feelings of isolation. We can relieve this suffering by showing everyone we meet

love, compassion and understanding. Love breaks down barriers and shows the interconnectedness we have with each other. It opens the heart and touches people at a deep level.

Delusions include strong desires and subtle cravings, destructive emotions and false impressions. The bodhisattva does not seek to stop delusions but rather to see them for what they are. This is what is meant by the phrase, 'I vow to cut through them.' The key to doing this is to not believe what you feel; to understand that it is just a feeling. This does not mean that you disbelieve, but rather that you look at all feelings objectively. When you feel a strong desire, it may feel as if your life depends upon fulfilling that desire but this is an illusion. Realizing that no one ever died from not fulfilling a desire allows you to observe the desire as if from a distance rather than being consumed by it. The same applies to emotions. Most emotions are tied to the past or the future and realizing this allows you to not buy into that emotion in the present.

The Dharma Gates refers to all the practices that lead to enlightenment. When life is easy, our practice can become less important to us, but challenging situations demand our full attention and focused practice. Our adversities are therefore a gift enabling us to approach one of the limitless Dharma Gates. The fourth vow acknowledges the fact that we are on a continual journey of learning and we will walk that journey steadfastly to its conclusion.

A bronze statue of Kuan Yin in Penang, Malaysia.

The Six Parmitas

The bodhisattva practises six *parmitas* or perfections of generosity, morality, patience, diligence, meditation and wisdom. The word parmita means 'that which has reached the other shore' and refers to practices on the path to enlightenment. Buddha taught them in this order from the easiest to the hardest with each practice forming the basis of the next one. For instance, it is impossible to practise morality without first practising generosity because greed and desire corrupt. We cannot truly act morally if we are still driven by attachment to objects and emotions.

Generosity

Generosity refers not only to being generous with material things, but also being generous with our time, our love and our understanding. It is about giving, seeking nothing in return. It is also about giving sound advice and helpful guidance when asked. Mindfulness is very important when giving so that our generosity is pure. For instance, to give an alcoholic a bottle of whisky is merely feeding another person's delusion. Likewise giving because we feel guilt, or we desire adulation is not practising in a true and honourable way.

Morality

In the Buddhist tradition morality refers to refraining from practices that have negative consequences for others or us and is classified by the Ten Non-virtues. These are further divided into three groups of speech, body and mind. The non-virtues of speech are lies, slander, gossip and harsh words (including swearing). The non-virtues of body are killing, stealing and sexual misconduct. The non-virtues of mind are attachment, wishing others harm and delusion. Practising morality presents us with many challenges because ultimately it is not just about words and actions but also about thought. For instance, it is one thing to refrain from sexual misconduct, but quite another to refrain from thinking about sexual misconduct.

Patience

Through practising morality we learn patience both with others and ourselves. Buddhism classifies

patience as follows: the patience of forgiveness, the patience of accepting suffering and the patience of virtuous behaviour. Practising morality teaches us to forgive ourselves when we fail and this in turn helps us to forgive those around us. It also teaches us inner strength and it is this that helps us to accept suffering and to have the courage to face challenging situations knowing that ultimately they will pass. Virtuous behaviour is born out of morality and can only be achieved through persistence and patience.

Diligence

Diligence is often translated as joyful effort because it is not only about steadfast and earnest application of practice but also about doing everything with pleasure. When we let go of duality, we begin to see spiritual significance in everything. Every moment is a doorway to enlightenment, filled with potential lessons. Even apparent setbacks can be embraced with joy once we understand that they merely fire our determination and strengthen our inner resolve. If we learn to approach all life with joyful effort we can be happy under all circumstances.

Meditation

It is interesting to note that Buddha places meditation as the penultimate parmita implying that it cannot truly be achieved until the previous four parmitas have been mastered. Meditation allows us to understand our true nature, but this cannot be achieved unless we have first let go of duality, desire, selfishness, pride and other delusions. The first four parmitas develop humility and it is only with humility that we can hope to achieve the goal of mastering the Self and realizing our buddhanature.

Wisdom

Wisdom is the highest of all perfections and the hardest to realize. It cannot be achieved without the previous five parmitas and yet it also feeds into them. The first five parmitas without wisdom develop only into egoism. Wisdom brings about the understanding of emptiness; that there is no 'I'. The realization that there is no 'I' arises through the act of meditation combined with the practice of the first four parmitas.

A true meditative state cannot be achieved while we hold desires and delusions within our heart; we must let them go.

'The path to enlightenment comes from wisdom and skilful means. The practice of the first four parmitas is the practice of skilful means. The last two parmitas reveal the practice of wisdom.'

BUDDHA

RINZAI: THE WAY OF THE KOANS

The Rinzai (Chinese: Linchi) School was named after Linchi (birth date unknown, d. 866 CE), one of the most influential of all Zen masters. Linchi was born in China at a time when the country was constantly at war with the invading Tartars and Turks and Zen teaching at the time was characterized by its warrior-like bluntness and forcefulness.

Linchi became a monk as a boy and as a young man studied under Zen Master Huang Po in a monastery with over five hundred monks. He would work in the fields in the morning, meditate in the afternoons and in the evenings help prepare food or baths for the older monks. His approach to life was simple; when he was eating he ate; when he was meditating he meditated. He did this for three years until the head monk, Mu Chou, noticing his pure and single-minded approach to monastic life, suggested he visited the master in his room and asked him what the fundamental principle of Buddhism was. Linchi stood before Master Huang Po and asked him this question. The master responded by hitting him with a six-foot pole. Again Linchi asked the same question and met the same response and a third time he asked and was once again hit.

Confused and disenchanted Linchi decided to give up monastic life and become a beggar in the hope that ordinary life might help him see the truth. Hearing of his plans Master Huang Po instructed him to go to Master Tu Yu's monastery assuring him he would find what he sought there. So Linchi went to Master Tu Yu and recounted what had happened. The master responded by telling Linchi that Huang Po had in fact been as kind to him as his own grandmother and that he was rather stupid if he could not understand this. At hearing these words Linchi was suddenly enlightened realizing that up

until then he had seen Buddhism as a teaching separate from himself. His question had sprung from illusion and Master Huang Po's hits had pointed to the truth of his own being. Later Linchi became famous for his forthright and abrupt style of teaching. He would often hit or shout at his students in order to wake them up from their illusions and bring them into a direct experience of the moment.

Like all Zen schools, the Rinzai tradition focused on meditation but also became noted for its use of koans. Koans are paradoxical riddles that have no rational answer. The purpose of the koan is to break the habitual thought processes of the mind; to short-circuit our logical thinking so that pure intuition can arise. The practice of koans is said to have originated from Master Chou Chou (778–897 CE) who had experienced his first awakening at a young age and had devoted his life to the study of Zen. At the age of 80 he was living in a small Zen temple in the town of Chouchou from which he took his name. One day a monk came to him and asked him the question, 'Does a dog have buddhanature?' Chou Chou replied, 'Mu' which means 'Nothing'. The Buddha taught that all sentient beings have buddhanature but Master Chou Chou did not answer, 'Yes, a dog has buddhanature,' but instead gave an answer that was neither 'Yes' nor 'No'. This was designed to prevent the monk from contemplating Buddhism rationally. Mu can be analysed at a rational level but its true meaning only becomes apparent when the rational mind lets go and the student becomes one with 'Mu'.

Rinzai Zen became popular in Japan in the 12th century and went through various ebbs and flows over the year but by the 17th century was in severe decline. It was resurrected by Hakuin (1686–1769), who was not only a renowned Zen Master but also a great poet, painter and sculptor. As a monk he spent four years meditating on the koan of whether a dog has buddhanature and at the end achieved what he was sure was enlightenment. When he shared this with his master he received an unenthusiastic response. Disappointed he visited other masters hoping to gain their recognition but not one gave it to him. At that time monks earned no wages and so when travelling relied upon gifts of food from the villages they visited. One day Hakuin was visiting a small village and he came to the house of an old woman to ask for rice. The woman was sweeping her floor at the time and refused to give him any rice. Hakuin was so self-absorbed about the lack of recognition for his enlightenment that he did not hear the woman and remained standing at her door as if she has said nothing to him. This infuriated the woman who hit him on the head with her broom knocking him to the ground. When he regained his senses his obsession was gone and he was instantly enlightened.

Hakuin went on to become a renowned master and resurrected the

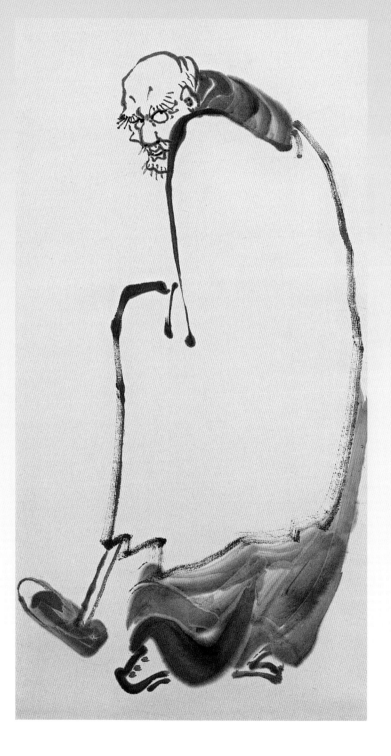

Zen Master Linchi, pictured here with a hoe, was noted for his abrupt style of teaching, which included hitting and shouting at his students.

strict study of koans organizing them into a course of study. He also added his own koans to those of previous masters, the most famous being, 'What is the sound of one hand clapping?' His method of teaching was to get students to solve koans through strict zazen (sitting meditation) practice followed by an interview (or *sanzen*) with their Zen master (in Japan called a *Roshi*). This tradition is still followed today in many Rinzai schools.

Koans are often presented as dialogues between a master and pupil and invariably a master's answer to a pupil's question defies logic. A student will contemplate a koan logically, sometimes for many years, until he finally lets go of logical thought. This is when the real work on the koan begins. He no longer thinks about the koan but it sits in his mind both day and night. He can neither answer it nor let it go. If he continues his practice he arrives at a point where he becomes one with the koan. He becomes the 'nothing' or the 'one hand'. With further practice the koan eventually disappears as his consciousness completely empties of thought. He is now close to enlightenment but must continue to persevere in his practice and remain totally empty. It now takes only a small spur to bring about enlightenment. The answer to the koan arrives unexpectedly from a sight, sound or perhaps an emotion. The enlightenment is instant and revolutionary. It cannot be adequately explained and is only perceived by those who are themselves enlightened.

Some Koans to Contemplate

- One day a monk came to Master Chou Chou and said, 'Master, I am still a novice, please show me the way.'
  Chou Chou asked, 'Have you eaten your breakfast yet?'
  The monk replied, 'Yes.'
  Then Chou Chou said, 'Go and wash your bowls.'

- Grandfather dies, father dies, son dies – this is good fortune.

- The wise don't strive to arrive.

- What did your face look like before your parents were born?

A student of koans learns to become the object of contemplation. In contemplating a running river, he would seek to see the river as motionless and himself as moving.

SOTO: THE WAY OF SILENT ILLUMINATION

The Soto (Chinese: Tsaotung) was named after its two founders Tungshan Liang-chieh (807–869 CE) and Tsaoshan Pen-chi (840–901 CE) who were master and disciple. In his youth Tungshan entered the Vinaya (Discipline) School of Buddhism and one day was reciting the Heart Sutra when he came to the line that says, 'There is no eye, ear, nose, tongue, body or mind.' Feeling his face he said to his teacher, 'I have eyes, ears, nose, tongue, body and mind; why does the sutra say there are none?' His teacher did not know the answer and said to him, 'I am not your teacher.' With this Tungshan left and went to study with the Zen masters where he gained his enlightenment.

Tungshan introduced the concept of the 'Five Ranks' to explain the path to enlightenment. The Five Ranks refer to the relationship between us and the Eternal or the relative and absolute. The relative or *Apparent* relates to the finite world of form, colour and other external qualities. The absolute or *Real* relates to the infinite world of emptiness, oneness and true nature. The Five Ranks are also represented in the form of five circles.

The first rank is *the Apparent within the Real* shown as a circle with the top half dark and the bottom half light. The dark half relates to the *Real.* This represents the sudden realization that although the things of daily life dominate our lives, they all come from the absolute. The absolute creates and sustains the real. This is the student's first glimpse into buddhanature.

The second rank is *the Real within the Apparent* shown as a circle with the top half light and the bottom half dark. Here the influence of the oneness becomes dominant and the differences between things disappear. One sees the infinite in every event, person and object. No longer is there a sense of 'I' and 'not I'; thought and the object of thought become one. This is where the student truly begins to listen, study and train.

The third rank is *the Coming from within the Real* represented as a white circle with a black dot in the middle. At this level both the mind and body fall away and for the first time we experience emptiness. This is the student's first awakening to the infinite.

The path of enlightenment is sometimes likened to the unfolding of a lotus flower.

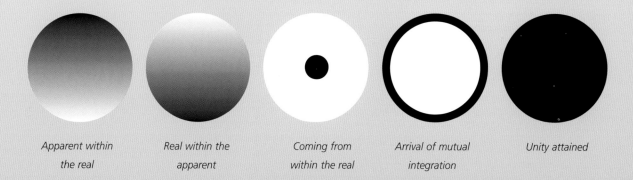

| Apparent within the real | Real within the apparent | Coming from within the real | Arrival of mutual integration | Unity attained |

The fourth rank is *the Arrival of Mutual Integration* shown as a white circle with a black border. At this stage the student gains a sense of inner knowing where the opinions of others and the opinions of Self are both forgotten. Everything is viewed as both individual and unique. Tungshan compared this rank to a lotus blooming within a fire and yet untouched by the fire. The student is totally immersed in the world, responding fully to its ebb and flow and yet is undisturbed by it.

The fifth rank is *Unity Attained* shown as a black circle. At this final stage form and emptiness interpenetrate. Thoughts of enlightenment or ignorance vanish. One no longer thinks about following the precepts in order to gain something or avoid losing something. All precepts are forgotten because they become part of our nature and are kept naturally and completely without thought. This is the place of the bodhisattva where the student is fully enlightened, unattached and free yet still very much within the world and a part of it.

Tungshan had 26 successors including Tsaoshan who spread his teaching throughout China, Yunchu (835–902 CE) who led a community of fifteen hundred people and produced 28 Enlightened Disciples and Sushan (837–909 CE) who produced 20 Enlightened Disciples. The lineage of Tungshan continued in China until the 17th century and continues to this day in Japan.

Just Sitting

Zen Master Hungshi (1091–1157) developed the ideas of the 'Five Ranks' into the Zen of Silent Illumination (Mokusho Zen). He taught that enlightenment could be achieved by sitting quietly in meditation without the mind focussing on anything

in particular. He extolled maintaining a firm posture while the mind contemplated its own stillness. The term 'Just Sitting' (Shikantaza) was introduced by Dogen, the founder of Japanese Soto.

Dogen studied with the Rinzai Zen Master Eisai and his successor, Myozen, for eight years and despite receiving his inka (the seal of a master), he still felt there was something lacking in his understanding. At the age of 24 he travelled with Myozen to China where he met and studied under Master Ju-ching. One day he heard the master scolding another monk for dozing off during zazen saying, 'the practice of zazen is the dropping away of body and mind. What can dozing accomplish?' On hearing this Dogen was suddenly enlightened. He returned to Japan and when asked what teachings he had brought back from his travels replied, 'I have returned empty-handed. I know only that the eyes are horizontal and the nose vertical.' Dogen set up a meditation hall in Kyoto and founded the Soto sect of Japan that still flourishes to this day.

Dogen was a prolific writer and gave detailed instructions for the correct practice of zazen that are still followed to this day. He also taught that one must not only be awakened in meditation but in all activities. In his 'Instructions for the Cook' he teaches about the mindful preparation of food and the importance of not dividing and separating between poor and fine food. Even when washing rice, the mind must be fully present, aware of the colour and smell of the rice and the coolness of the water. Rice,

he taught, should be washed without discrimination, judgment or expectation. Every action, no matter how mundane, is sacred and can lead one to enlightenment. This teaching led to the creation of rituals for all aspects of Zen practice.

Rituals remind Zen students of the need to be awake and present in each and every moment. They are an acknowledgement of the sacredness of all things and the interconnectedness of all creation. As well as rituals for making rice, entering the zendo (meditation hall) and performing zazen, many other rituals were created that became the foundation of the Do (the Way). Rituals were thus created for each of the Do's including Chado, the Way of Tea, Kado, the Way of Flower-Arranging, and Budo, the Way of the Warrior. These rituals brought grace and beauty into Zen practice.

Zen practice in the Soto School is very ritualized to this day and following daily rituals continually reminds students of the possibility of enlightenment in every moment. The Soto School also places great emphasis on paying respect to the previous Zen masters and patriarchs who have transmitted the teachings over the centuries. This acknowledges the fact that without the work and selfless discipline of those who have gone before, there would be no Zen tradition to follow. Consequently in modern Japanese Zen temples there is the daily recitation of the names of all the past masters all the way back to Shakyamuni Buddha (the historical Buddha, Siddhartha).

'Wash away the dust and dirt of subjective thinking…then the mind is open, brightly shining, without boundaries.'

HUNGSHI

Silent illumination teaches that the path to enlightenment can be achieved through the act of just sitting in meditation.

ZAZEN – ZEN MEDITATION

'When man sits,
then the coarse passions subside
and the luminous mind
arises in awareness:
Thus consciousness is illuminated.'

MEISTER ECKHART

ZEN MEDITATION

'When someone practises zazen, even if only for twenty minutes, it is as if the whole world were practising zazen.'

DOGEN

Zazen is a form of meditation used in the practice of Zen Buddhism. Without zazen there would be no Zen. All schools of Buddhism practise meditation, as do many other spiritual traditions, but what makes zazen unique is that it is practised with the eyes open and the mind fully aware. There is no drifting off into visions or daydreams but a full and complete awareness of the wonder of creation. In its true form, zazen is the manifestation of supreme enlightenment. When mastered, zazen can be practised anywhere and everywhere: when sitting in a zendo (meditation hall), when hanging out the washing or when driving a car. Zazen is the realization of buddhanature.

When we study Zen, whether it is through reading books or as a pupil of a great Zen master, all we are doing is studying Zen. We can read all the sutras (the teachings of Buddha), listen to the teachings of the thousands of Zen masters who have lived before us, study body, mind and art, but without zazen we will not find enlightenment. There are many ways to describe the practice of zazen such as just sitting, following the breath and being at one with the Self, but these are just descriptions. The true wonder of zazen can only be found in the application and practice of these descriptions. When we sit in zazen we become one with the Buddha and we become one with all of the Zen masters who have ever lived or will ever live. This is because enlightenment is the realization of our true nature, a coming to know our true Self. Once Self is realized, the whole universe becomes Self and past, present and future become as one.

The Ten Ox-herding Pictures (pages 46–55) describe the journey a student takes when practising zazen. It is a journey of many steps and yet a journey of but one step. In the beginning the student wanders through the high mountains and deep waters searching for something. He sees the high mountains as high mountains and the deep waters as deep waters. As his practice deepens he loses the sense of Self and the mountains cease being mountains, the waters cease being waters. As his practice deepens further and matures, the mountains once again become mountains and the waters once again become waters. However, the experience of creation by the beginner is not the experience of creation by the mature student, but in both cases the high mountains and deep waters remain the same. It is not creation that changes but we who change.

In the final Ox-herding picture the student re-enters the world as an enlightened being and his whole life becomes a walking meditation.

He is in a perpetual state of zazen and everything he does is done with beauty and grace. This sense of living zazen is what is at the heart of the Japanese arts or 'Do's'. The word 'Do'(Chinese: Tao) means 'the Way' and to walk this 'Way' is to be a true artist. Hence there is an art to tea-making (Chado), to flower-arranging (Kado), to fighting (Budo) and writing (Shodo) and each of these arts, when practised correctly, is a form of zazen. Anyone can make tea, arrange flowers, learn martial arts or write, but it is only when the practice of these arises out of the core of zazen that they become the true practice of the Way.

Zazen is not something to be played with or taken lightly. To choose to practise zazen is to make a commitment to understand the true nature of Self. The moment you begin practising, you are realizing your buddhanature, whether you are aware of it or not. It is without doubt one of the most potentially life-changing experiences you will ever encounter. It will take you deeper inside of your Self than you have ever gone before. How deep? To infinity and beyond!

'Mind and body dropped off…
this state should be experienced by everyone.'

DOGEN

Prayer is an important part of daily practice for Zen monks.
These monks are praying at Throssel Hole Abbey in
Northumberland, England.

WHY DO WE MEDITATE?

'If you misunderstand your mind, you are an ordinary mortal;
if you understand your mind, you are a sage.'

JAKUSHITSU

Everyone seeks happiness in their lives but all too often the happiness we find is fleeting. This is because most people seek happiness in external things such as a loving relationship, good food, fine wine, fame and fortune. However, true and lasting happiness is not dependant upon external stimuli but is a state of mind, an attitude to life. Happiness is the perfect practice of life's art and because it arises from within, it can only be achieved through knowing one's Self. When we live externally, we live in duality; so happiness begets sadness, which begets happiness and so on. When we realize that we are not separate individuals, but that everything is interconnected, duality disappears and real happiness is realized.

Meditation takes us away from the external and introduces us to the internal. The external world is a sea of waves that tosses us from pillar to post. Meditation gives us the opportunity to be at one with the sea; to become the sea and to flow in perfect harmony. It is not about finding something new, but about rediscovering something that is as old as the universe. Through meditation we change our perception of our Self and in doing so change our relationship with all things. We begin a journey to find the real meaning to life, the reason why we are here. We stop differentiating between good and bad, right and wrong and learn to accept each and every moment and appreciate its innate beauty and perfection.

Buddha described meditation as single-pointed mind and explained that it is achieved in three stages. Firstly we change our external and internal environment. Externally we create a quiet and safe environment in which to meditate, one that allows us the time and space to be still. Internally we change our attitude to life by ceasing to crave what we don't

have, being content with what we do have, giving up pointless activities and practising morality. Secondly we practise meditation in the correct manner. This involves maintaining the correct posture and developing concentration as described in the following pages. This leads us to the third stage, which is the achievement of alertness and mental clarity. Our mind no longer wanders, tossed around by the ebb and flow of life, but remains calm, clear and stable under all circumstances. Once this third stage has been achieved, wisdom naturally arises and we become a sage. Delusions dissolve and we are elevated into buddhanature.

It can take many years of practice to achieve this third stage but once it happens, everything about life changes. Stress and anxiety fade away to be replaced by faith and joy. You no longer hold beliefs but

Meditation can open one's mind to a deeper appreciation of the beauty of creation and the wonder of being a part of that beauty.

instead have an inner knowing that maintains and sustains inner peace and harmony. You are at one with the world and see the beauty in all things. Gone are the desires for happiness, for you are living in heaven on Earth. Happiness is no longer a concept or a dream, but a moment-by-moment reality. You accept everything and everyone, understanding that all is exactly as it needs to be. This third stage is achievable by anyone and everyone. It is not dependant upon age, race or creed. You don't even have to be a Buddhist to achieve it. It is who you really are, what you were born to be. It is the gift of life and your destiny should you choose it.

SITTING LIKE A MOUNTAIN

'From time immemorial the mountains have been the dwelling place of the great sages. Wise ones and sages have all made the mountains their own chambers, their own body and mind.'

DOGEN

The first step in the correct application of zazen is the posture. The idea of 'sitting like a mountain' is that you remain in a perfectly still position during the whole of your zazen session whether it lasts five minutes or an hour. This invariably presents a great challenge for many Westerners but one that is well worth the perseverance to achieve. By stilling the body, you will find it much easier to still the mind and maintain your mindful awareness. Traditionally one sits on a single, round cushion about 5–8 cm (2–3 in) in height in the Lotus position, called *kekka* in Japanese, or in the Half Lotus.

The Lotus position is achieved by placing the right foot on the left thigh and the left foot on the right thigh. In the Half-Lotus, one foot rests on the opposite thigh and the other foot rests underneath the opposite thigh. Both these positions can be difficult for some people to achieve so an even easier variation is the Quarter-Lotus in which one foot lies on the opposite thigh and the other rests under the opposite knee. All three variations of the Lotus position are done sitting on a cushion so that both knees are in contact with the floor. An equally acceptable position is kneeling, called *seiza* in Japanese. In this position a cushion is often placed between the buttocks and the legs. One final variation is sitting on a chair. The chair should be firm with a straight back. Sit forward on the chair so that you use your back to support yourself, with your legs crossed at the ankles so that your knees are lower than your pelvis and with both feet touching the floor. Whatever position you choose, seek to find stillness within it.

The Sitting Position

1 Once sitting, centre your spine by gently swaying from side to side in decreasing arcs. Now straighten and align your spine by imagining a golden thread attached to your crown and pulling you up. Once this is done, relax, as your back should be erect but not rigid or tense. Your head should rest squarely on your spine with your chin slightly tucked in. This will bring your ears parallel with your shoulders and the tip of your nose centred over your navel.

2 Sit with your eyes looking down at a 45-degree angle gazing in a relaxed and unfocused manner at the floor a metre (three to four feet) in front of you. If you are sitting in front of a wall, look 'through' the wall to where the floor would be.

3 Keep your lips closed with the tongue gently resting on the upper palette behind the top front teeth. This connects the two major acupuncture meridians that run up the spine and down the front of the body. Swallow any saliva in the mouth, breathe in through the nose and out once through the mouth. This creates a slight vacuum in your mouth that reduces salivation. Then begin breathing in and out through the nose.

4 Place your right hand palm up across your lower belly with the left palm also facing up and resting on the right hand with the middle knuckles slightly overlapping. The thumbs should touch at the tips in a straight line so that their shape forms neither a mountain nor a valley. If you are left-handed you reverse the hand positions. This hand position is called 'the cosmic mudra'. In this position you should remain perfectly still throughout your period of zazen.

ZEN BREATHING

Throughout the practice of zazen the eyes remain open to help prevent distracting mental images from arising and to guard against falling asleep during practice. Zen Master Dogen suggests that one 'thinks of not-thinking' and this often presents the greatest challenge to those new to zazen. Many people find it very difficult to meditate without a subject so initially one is taught to focus on the breathing. Most Westerners do not breathe properly and use only a small portion of their lung capacity. They tend to breathe through the mouth and use only the chest to power the breathing, making it shallow. If your breathing is shallow you will quickly tire and lose your focus during zazen so it is very important to learn the correct way to breathe in zazen.

Breathing Meditation 1

This meditation is a good way to focus the mind and clear away distracting thoughts. It is usually practised by those who are new to zazen as a preparation for deeper meditation. It should initially be practised for a maximum of five minutes only but can be done several times a day. You can also use it as a means of centring and calming your Self whenever you feel worried or stressed.

Make sure you are wearing loose, comfortable clothes and will not be disturbed during your practice. You might even wish to unplug the telephone. Choose a quiet, uncluttered space away from draughts.

1 Sit in the correct posture and centre your spine by gently swaying from side to side in decreasing arcs. Look down at a 45-degree angle with your eyes gazing unfocused at the floor.

2 Close your mouth, breathe in through your nose and exhale once through your mouth.

3 Start counting the breaths from one to ten as follows: breathe in (one), breathe out (two), in (three), out (four)...in (nine), out (ten). Then start counting from one again.

4 When your mind wanders or you lose count, begin counting from one again and continue.

5 If frustration arises let it go. Persevere in your practice until you can do a full five minutes of focused counting without being distracted by other thoughts.

Breathing should be slow and deep through the nose and powered by the diaphragm. This deep, abdominal breathing uses the full capacity of the lungs and thus reduces the frequency of breathing. Most Westerners, when relaxed, take between 14 and 20 breaths every minute. An experienced zazen practitioner will take only six to ten breaths every minute. When inhaling, allow the stomach and diaphragm to expand so that you are breathing into your belly. Do not force your stomach out but just focus on drawing the breath deeply. When exhaling, the diaphragm and stomach gently contract as if your belly were a sponge being gently squeezed from the bottom up. Do not pause for any length of time between breaths and never hold the breath.

Breathing in zazen should be slow and relaxed flowing naturally in and out. This deep, relaxed breathing boosts the circulation and calms the nervous system making it easier to calm the mind while remaining alert. It can take a little time to get used to correct breathing and perseverance is needed to maintain it in a relaxed way. To help calm the mind you might like at first to focus on two simple points. When breathing in, clear the mind of all thoughts and focus your full attention on the stomach. When breathing out, breathe out all distractions and stress.

Relaxed deep breathing helps to calm the mind and body making it possible for one to sit in zazen for long periods of time without tiring.

Zazen

When one begins to practise breathing meditation, the aim is to count up to ten and then start again at one and to do this without the interruption of any distracting thoughts. In reality, however, you will find that you rarely reach five breaths before a thought pops into your head. The only way to deal with this problem is to keep on practising this meditation while letting all thoughts go as soon as they arise. If you feel frustrated be aware that this is just another kind of thought and let it go also. It can take many weeks or months of daily practice before you truly achieve uninterrupted breathing meditation. If you find that you do manage to reach ten breaths, check that you have been alert and mindful during the whole process and have not become 'lost' in the counting.

The successful practice of zazen is not a quick process. If you think you have achieved success in only a few days you are most probably kidding your Self. The ego is always attached to outcomes and so will seek 'success' as quickly as possible. This is yet another kind of thinking that must be released if you are to move deeper in your practice. Remember that one of the non-virtues of mind is delusion so do not be tempted to lie to your Self and imagine you are further on in your practice than you actually are. Only when you can actually achieve a full five minutes of counting the breaths in and out up to ten and starting again are you ready to move on to the next stage.

Zen gardens, like this one in Kyoto, Japan, are an external expression of the state of mind of zazen – calm and simple.

Breathing Meditation 2

When one first practises Zen meditation, the aim is to focus and calm the mind. Once you can spend five minutes concentrating only on the breath you are ready to go deeper in your practice. This meditation, when practised regularly, will allow you to take the calmness of your mind and allow it to spread throughout your body. As mental challenges arise, you can practise letting go and by doing so you will release tension held within the body. Practise for a maximum of five minutes until you can consistently remain in a meditative state before proceeding to longer sessions.

1 Sit in the correct posture and resolve not to move at all during the whole of this meditation. Follow all the preparatory steps until you are ready to begin your meditation.

2 Start counting the breaths with each inhalation and exhalation counting as one as follows: breathe in and out (one), in and out (two)…in and out (ten).

3 Remain fully aware and mindful during the whole breath, not just when you count.

4 When your mind wanders or thoughts arise begin counting at one again.

5 If you reach a count of ten, begin back at one again.

Do not cheat, as it serves no purpose. The aim of this meditation is to clear and calm the mind, not to succeed in the shortest possible time. Have faith in your practice. With perseverance you will succeed. Do not allow frustrations and disappointments to deter you. Every time your mind wanders, understand that it gives you another opportunity to practise letting go. Once you can truly achieve this successfully for five minutes, extend your meditation time to ten minutes.

ZAZEN

When practising zazen all distractions must be firmly restrained. When meditating under the guidance of a master, a student who shows signs of distractions or tiredness will be quickly brought back into focus and alertness.

The master shouting at the student or dealing them a sharp blow, usually to an acupuncture point on the shoulders, brings the pupil swiftly back into focus. The response of the student is to humbly thank the master and return to zazen with even more diligence. This is not done to bring about obedience or submission but to help the student remain alert and to loosen up tense muscles.

According to Zen Master Dogen, the practice of zazen is the realization of buddhanature. Practice and realization are not separate for to think of them this way is to think in duality. Think only of non-thinking. To do this one must step beyond the duality of non-thinking and thinking, being free in the moment without weariness or confusion. Zazen is simply the easy and pleasant practice of a Buddha.

A Zen master holding a kyosaku which is used to strike meditating monks between the neck and right shoulder to assist concentration.

Zazen Meditation

Once you have mastered the two Zen breathing meditations, you are ready to begin formal zazen practice. Zazen, when practised daily, will take you on a journey within yourself. Every time you practise the experience will be unique; each time taking you a little further on your spiritual path. Begin practising for five minutes and then proceed gradually on to longer sessions of up to an hour. Choose a room free of distractions or sit in front of a plain wall.

1 Adopt the correct posture and prepare for meditation, resolving to not move until the session is complete.

2 Breathe slowly and naturally from the belly and focus only on being aware.

3 If thoughts arise, let them flow in and out with ease. Do not be taken by any thought but remain totally in the moment.

4 If you experience discomfort or pain, just sit with it and it will dissipate of its own accord.

5 Try not to judge thoughts that arise as good or bad, right or wrong. Just observe them as if from a distance. Watch them come and go.

6 You may at times find that you have no thoughts; this is a moment of pure awareness. However the second you realize this you are thinking again and have lost it. Ultimately you are seeking to be aware without thinking.

7 When your session is over, sit for a moment to allow the circulation to fully flow in your legs. As you get up and move into other activities, try to maintain a state of mindfulness and awareness.

SITTING WITH KOANS

One day a Zen Master was lying on his deathbed surrounded by his most loyal students. His oldest student said to him, 'Master, in all your many years of Zen practice, what is the most important thing you have learned?' The master smiled and replied, 'I do not know' and then peacefully passed away. All the students looked sad and confused except the oldest student who burst out laughing. Why did the student laugh?

Zen is notoriously cryptic and students of Zen often spend many years in serious contemplation of its nature. However, when an enlightenment occurs, it is not unusual for it to be announced with spontaneous laughter. This is because the realization is so beautifully simple and, once realized, so glaringly obvious that the student laughs at his own blindness. So once again we ask ourselves the question, what was so glaringly obvious to the student in the above story that caused his great mirth? After a life dedicated to Zen, it appears that the master did not know what the most important thing he had learned was. How could this be; did death bring confusion to him or the ultimate clarity?

If the master had been a poet, he might have said, 'I do *poetry* know' or if he were an artist his response would have been, 'I do *art* know'. Being a Zen Master be said, 'I do *not* know'. This is the essence of the koan 'Mu'. Mu means 'not' or 'nothing'. The master knew nothing! He knew *not* right or wrong, *not* good or bad, *not* fair or unfair. Duality had vanished and all he knew was 'not'.

When enlightenment occurs, it is often accompanied by laughter as the student realizes the beautiful simplicity of truth and how it is so obvious.

Koan Meditation 1

Koans challenge our perceptions of reality, they invite us to look deeper within ourselves and find new ways of seeing life. But in order to take hold of new perceptions, one first has to empty the consciousness of old perceptions. This exercise is a tool for helping this process.

1 Sit in the correct posture, follow the preparation for meditation and resolve to not move until the session is over.

2 Calm your mind by counting the breaths for five minutes.

3 Sit with the koan 'Mu' by saying to yourself silently, 'nothing'. Keep repeating 'nothing' in your mind.

4 When thoughts arise reflect that they are nothing but thoughts arising from the ego.

5 Don't think intellectually, just stay with 'nothing'.

6 Be aware that irritation may arise but this too is nothing.

7 If you find your mind empty of thought, just sit with it until the mind wanders and then return to nothing.

8 Now, in this moment all is nothing.

9 When you finish your meditation, which can last up to 30 minutes, keep this awareness of nothing in your mind.

The Art of Letting Go

Zen is all about *letting go*; letting go of duality, the ego, intellectual thoughts and judgments. The opposite of *letting go* is of course 'holding on' and it is holding on that is at the root of all suffering. When a relationship comes to an end, if we try to hold on to it we suffer from sadness, regret and sentimentality. If parents try to hold on to their children when they grow up, it not only causes them to suffer but it might also result in causing suffering to their children. Often in life you have to love others enough to let them go. This is the secret to unconditional love.

In life we are continually challenged to let go of both the past and future and even if we continually fail to do so, there is one *letting go* that we all must do and that is to let go of life itself. Part of the magic of life is its impermanence and death is the ultimate *letting go*. A famous Zen koan/proverb states, 'He who dies before he dies, does not die when he dies.' Part of what this means is that if we can learn to let go of things while we are alive, the letting go of life itself becomes much easier. In Zen, when one achieves full enlightenment, the cycle of life, death and rebirth is transcended; so if one learns to die in life, death is no longer death but transformation and can be embraced without fear.

'Death is life and life is death.'

BUDDHIST PROVERB

These monks are attending a memorial ceremony at Bukkokuji Temple, Japan. Zen teaches that to truly understand life, one must truly understand death.

Koan Meditation 2

Despite our best efforts to let go, still the ego holds on to fear-based worries, anxieties and self-doubt. However, if we can learn to face our fears and let them go, even death loses its fear and becomes just another doorway into a new understanding of the wonder of life.

1 Sit in the correct posture and resolve not to move until the session is over.

2 Calm your mind by counting the breaths for five minutes.

3 Seek to awaken to your true nature by contemplating the phrase 'He (or she) who dies before he (or she) dies, does not die when he (or she) dies.'

4 Reflect that all suffering originates in holding on and seek to 'die' to all thoughts of the past and future.

5 As thoughts arise, watch them as if from a distance fade away into nothing.

6 If fear arises, let that go also, understanding that it is no more than a feeling.

7 Seek only to be fully aware of the moment.

8 When you have finished your meditation, be aware of letting go as you go about your daily life, especially when you begin to feel stressed.

WALKING WITH AWARENESS

When studying in a Zen monastery, many days are devoted to practising intensive zazen throughout the day under the guidance of a teacher (roshi). These days of spiritual collectedness are called *sesshins*. They often start with an early rise, a period of zazen followed by a simple breakfast and then more zazen. Usually later in the morning there will be either a lecture by the roshi (called a teishō) or a private one-to-one interview between master and student (called a *dokusan*). This will be followed by more periods of zazen with breaks for lunch and supper.

A sesshin may consist of up to fifteen 30-minute periods of zazen interspersed with ten-minute breaks. During these breaks a special kind of walking is practised called kin-hin. This walking zazen allows the student to gently exercise his limbs while maintaining mindfulness. It is also a step towards practising Zen in daily life.

Teishō literally means 'to offer a discourse'. In Japanese tei means 'to offer' or 'to present' and shō means 'to discourse'. Dukusan is made up of two Japanese words, doku which means 'alone' or 'single' and san, which means 'going to a higher one'. This dialogue between master and student helps to direct the student's intent.

'Even if you are in a high place, don't forget you may fall. Even if you are safe, don't forget danger. Even though you are alive today, don't assume you will be alive tomorrow.'

DOGEN

When one walks through life with awareness, all of nature becomes vibrant with energy and not a single flower blossom goes unnoticed.

Walking Zazen

This walking meditation is not only valuable when practising intensive zazen, but also as an exercise in itself to help calm the mind and relax the body.

1 Form your left hand into a fist with the thumb enclosed by the fingers.

2 Place the fist on your solar plexus with the knuckles facing up.

3 Lightly arch the fingers of your right hand over the back of your left fist keeping your forearms horizontal to the ground.

4 Direct your gaze to a point on the floor about 3 m (10 ft) in front of you.

5 Step forward with your left heel and simultaneously lift your right heel.

6 Transfer your weight fully to your left foot and lift your right foot completely.

7 Step forward with your right foot placing the heel down first and simultaneously lift your left heel, and so on.

8 Walk in a square or circle keeping your breathing relaxed and your mind alert but clear.

9 Let any thoughts flow in and out of your mind without becoming attached to them.

10 Continue this practice for up to ten minutes.

JUST SITTING

The practice of Zen should not be limited to sessions of zazen meditation but should filter into all aspects of daily life. Approaching life from a perspective of calm, mindful clarity not only helps us to navigate life's challenges successfully, but has a knock-on effect with everyone we encounter. Calmness is contagious and when we encounter people who are over-excited or deeply stressed, the persona we greet them with can have profound and positive consequences. By remaining calm when all around us is chaos, we bring a stabilizing influence to situations. So often we get taken along by other people's emotions and in doing so we compound problems rather than solve them. This is where the practice of Zen in daily life can be of great benefit.

How you start your day tends to dictate the flavour of the rest of the day. If you get up late, bolt down a quick breakfast and rush out of the door to work you are already suffering from stress. The strain that hurrying puts on our minds and bodies can be immense and not only puts us under stress but saps our energy making it even harder to think and act with calmness and clarity. Why not try getting up 15 minutes earlier and spending five minutes just sitting in quiet contemplation before using the other extra ten minutes to eat breakfast in a calm and unhurried manner? You will be amazed at the difference this makes to your energy levels throughout the day.

You can also practise 'just sitting' in a whole host of different circumstances throughout your day. When stuck in a traffic jam, rather than sigh with impatience, why not accept the situation and make the best of it by just sitting and emptying your mind of thought? Likewise if you find yourself in a queue, you can even practise 'just sitting' while standing in line. Just sitting means adopting the same attitude of inner calm combined with total alertness that you do when practising zazen. You can do it while cooking, cleaning, washing-up and driving. The mind, like a wine glass, is designed to be filled and emptied. If you had a glass of wine and never drank it, it would soon become stale and unpalatable. If thoughts are allowed to flow in and out of our minds our thinking is always fresh. Hold on to thoughts and our thinking becomes stale and our personality more unpalatable.

If you want to be always fresh and vibrant in life, you need to regularly empty your mind so that new thoughts can arise. Throughout the day it is valuable to regularly take time out to just sit. Instead of using a break time to fill up with a stimulant such as coffee, why not do the opposite and use the time to empty your mind? Life is a journey, not a race and those who treat it like a race tend to finish it much earlier. We live in a world where no-one appears to have enough time, especially to devote to themselves, but this is an illusion caused by too much doing and too much thinking. Do less and think less and you will almost certainly achieve much more.

Zen is all about living moment by moment in an alert but meditative state. The practice of zazen helps us to get used to doing this but is itself useless if we cannot carry it forward into all our daily activities. Zen is not a stale old religion, but a vibrant and life-giving way of being. As the Zen proverb says: 'Flowing water never goes stale,' so why not choose to flow through life rather than rush about from one crisis to another? In this way you learn to appreciate life rather than watch it run by you.

Even the most mundane of acts, such as hanging out the washing, take on a new meaning when approached from a Zen perspective.

GOING ON RETREAT

Attending a Zen retreat is powerful and challenging way to deepen your experience of Zen. Retreats usually last a week and are conducted mostly in silence. A typical day begins with an early rise and consists mainly of periods of zazen and walking meditation. Students take simple meals together, eaten in silence, and there are also one or two work periods when cooking, cleaning, chopping wood or other work is done, again performed in mindful silence. Often mid-morning the teacher will give a lecture, which may be a commentary on passages from ancient Zen texts or practical instructions on the correct practice and state of mind one is trying to develop. There are also opportunities for students to have a one-to-one interview with the teacher (*dokusan*) where one can discuss any difficulties being encountered or questions that may arise.

Retreats offer many challenges that enable us to go much deeper into ourselves, not least of which is the experience of pain. This is not only the pain of physical discomfort from extended periods of sitting in one position but also the mental pain of being still and silent. The physical pain, if embraced, eases with time but the mental pain can be much more of a challenge. Silence and stillness takes us into ourselves because we are not able to be distracted by sharing or listening to the interesting stories that Westerners like to talk about. We have to learn to accept our own company and make friends with who we really are. Silence brings clarity, showing us the misconceptions we have about the emotions we carry and about ourselves. When in silence you have to face yourself; there is no means of running away, and this gives you an opportunity to see yourself clearly, warts and all.

Another challenge is tiredness. This can be because we have been working too hard before coming on retreat but more often it is a form of escapism, a refusal to face who we really are. Often, as soon as we begin to sit in zazen, tiredness descends like a cloud and we find ourselves feeling heavy, sleepy and unable to concentrate. The best way to counter this initially is to focus on the correct posture. Every time we begin to slouch, imagining a golden thread pulling us up from the crown of the head will straighten the back and bring back alertness and clarity. Another important factor is our intent. Why did we come on this retreat and what are we running away from? If we still cannot focus we can remember the impermanence of life and that death can come at any moment. Would we really be so sleepy if our next breath were our last?

Perhaps the challenge that arises most throughout the whole of the retreat is calming the mind. As soon as we sit the mind starts racing. Firstly sensations of the body fill our consciousness. We feel discomfort in our legs or, even worse, parts of our body begin to itch. The more you focus on the itch, the worse it gets and the urge to move and scratch becomes almost unbearable. The only answer is to relax in the moment. Eventually the feelings pass and we calm down only to find our mind filled with irrelevant thoughts and images. We think about the past, the future, worries, grievances, food and sex. Paranoia arises as we wonder what the teacher and our fellow students think about us. When in silence, we can read a thousand implications into a glance from the teacher or brief eye contact with another student during break-time. Sometimes we relive painful events from the past over and over again wishing we had acted differently to avoid the pain or creating devious and cruel ways to exact revenge on those we perceive have hurt us. At other times we endlessly judge ourselves and others. Am I sitting right? Did I answer the questions of the teacher correctly? Is the teacher treating me fairly? When is it time to eat dinner? On and on we go until we finally begin to let go and focus only on the meditation.

There are many different kinds of Zen retreat available to students. Some take place in monasteries, others in places of natural beauty.

A Japanese Retreat

A Japanese retreat tends to be more formal than other retreats. Students usually wear black loose-fitting clothes or a black Zen robe. There are set ways of eating, entering and exiting the meditation hall (Zendo), preparing to sit and finishing a period of zazen. A bell is rung to indicate the beginning and end of a period of zazen. At the beginning of zazen the bell is rung three times, when walking meditation starts it is rung twice and at the end of the session it is rung once.

During zazen a person walks around the room holding a stick, which is used to strike you on the shoulder should you show signs of sleepiness, tension or loss of concentration. In some centres this is done automatically while in others it is only done at the request of the student. If a student requests the stick (*kyosaku*), he or she signals to the stick holder (*jikido*) by putting their palms together as they approach. The stick is placed on the right shoulder as the student lowers his head to the left. After being hit, the student sits up straight again and bows to the jikido who bows back.

The retreats are usually held in complete silence with no eye contact between students. As well as the usual interviews, the teacher also conducts ceremonies throughout the day including the recitation of the particular lineage connected to the retreat. The group chants the name of each past master in the lineage and bows at each name. This kind of retreat tends to be very intense but a potentially life-changing experience as it pushes students to let go and step beyond their perceived limitations. They are not for the faint-hearted and require a strong intent and self-dedication to be successfully carried out. This kind of retreat is not recommended for novices.

The Daily Programme of a Japanese Zen Sesshin

4.00	Wake up
4.20–5.00	Zazen
5.00–6.00	Ceremony
6.00–6.40	Breakfast
6.40–7.30	Work period (*samu*)
7.30–8.10	Zazen
8.10–8.30	*Kin-hin* (zazen whilst walking) and a ten-minute break
8.30–9.40	*Teishō* (lecture by the Zen Master) and a ten-minute break
9.40–10.50	Zazen followed by *Kin-hin* (including opportunities for *dokusan*)
10.50–11.30	Zazen
11.30–11.45	Ceremony
11.45–12.30	Lunch
12.30–14.00	Rest
14.00–15.00	Zazen followed by *Kin-hin* (including opportunities for *dokusan*)
15.00–15.10	Break
15.10–15.50	Zazen
15.50–16.30	Zazen
16.30–16.45	Ceremony
16.45–17.40	Supper
17.40–18.20	Rest
18.20–19.00	Zazen
19.00–19.20	*Kin-hin* and a ten-minute break
19.20–20.00	Zazen
20.00–20.20	*Kin-hin* and a ten-minute break
20.20–21.00	Zazen
21.00	Tea followed by sleep

Some retreats in Japan require participants to make a considerable journey to a monastery in the hills before the real inner journey begins.

ZEN AND THE MARTIAL ARTS

'You must concentrate upon and consecrate yourself wholly to each day, as though a fire were raging in your hair.'

INSTRUCTIONS TO A MEDIEVAL SAMURAI

THE WAY OF THE WARRIOR

It may seem a contradiction to link the peaceful way of Zen with the fighting spirit of martial arts but they have much in common. They have identical stages of progression. Firstly, there is a period of conscious practice where the will is active as the student seeks to find inner peace. Secondly, the student learns to let go and be at peace and he becomes an assistant to the master helping other students in their practice. Finally he becomes a master himself and walks into the world a truly free human being.

The Japanese term for martial arts is budo (*bu* meaning 'war' and *do* meaning 'the way') and covers all the Japanese martial arts including *kendo* (the way of the sword), *kyodo* (the way of archery), *judo* (the way of adaptability) and *aikido* (the way of harmony). However, the Japanese word *bu* not only means 'war' but also means 'to cease the struggle' or 'to sheathe the sword'. This apparent contradiction shows the true essence of budo. One does not become a master of budo by learning techniques to defeat your foes, but by following the way that defeats the Self and brings inner peace. Budo is the combination of Zen and the martial arts. Without Zen, martial arts cease to be arts and become merely fighting sports.

As Japanese martial arts have moved to the West, they have had to adapt to the Western mind. Many Westerners do not understand that only practice makes a master and seek reassurance that they are making progress on their path. To fulfil this need, different coloured belts were introduced into martial arts such as judo to denote different levels of achievement. Originally there was only one colour of belt: white. When a student was accepted by a master he wore a white belt, which was never washed. As he progressed over the years, the belt would become marked with dirt and stains. After many years of practice, the belt would no longer be white but black with dirt. This is where the idea of a 'black belt' denoting a master originated.

> 'In the spirit of Zen and Budo everyday life becomes the contest... that is the place for mastery of the self.'
>
> ZEN MASTER DESHIMARU

Samurai ethics were portrayed in the Kabuki theatre. This Japanese print shows the actor Ichikawa Kuzo in the role of Sanzo. He is dancing in honour of the god Daikoko.

BUDO WISDOM

One of the founding concepts in budo is called *sutemi*. *Sute* means 'to abandon or throw away' and *mi* means 'the body'. This, just as in Zen, means letting go of the physical body with its desires and attachments so that one can move naturally and unconsciously. In martial arts, if you think then you have already lost. In budo, consciousness and action are one and the same and this can only be achieved when the ego is vanquished.

We all understand this concept and even practise it in our daily lives. When learning to drive a car, at first you have to think about all sorts of things and your driving is erratic. You think about your feet on the pedals and forget to steer properly or you look only ahead and forget to check in your mirrors for vehicles behind. If you continued behaving in this way you would never pass your driving test because you would be a danger to yourself, all other road users and pedestrians. Fortunately, with practice, the actions become unconscious and you steer, accelerate, brake and look both forwards and behind without having to think about it. When you can do all these complicated moves without the conscious mind intervening, you become a good driver. If you take this training further and learn to drive a Formula One car you might even become a master driver.

The practice of Budo and Zen require us to become so familiar with it that we become one with the practice. When you begin sitting in zazen there is often pain in the legs, shoulders, neck or back. You ask yourself, 'Is my posture right?' You have to adjust your posture by straightening your back, pulling your chin in, stretching the neck and breathing in a deep and relaxed way. Later, as your practice deepens, you do all these things naturally without thinking. Likewise maintaining the right attitude initially takes regular practice and we frequently fall into old ways of thinking. In Budo you must learn to remain composed at all times and not allow fear to take away your clarity. Even in the midst of defeat, one who has truly mastered fear may well become victorious. It is the same in Zen. When right attitude and mindfulness become natural, even the most challenging and extreme of situations fail to move us from calmness and clarity.

Hachiman, the god of war and patron of all warriors, is one of the most popular Shinto deities and almost half the shrines throughout Japan are dedicated to him.

Defeat in Victory: A Zen Story

One day a samurai was involved in a brawl and found himself fighting a commoner. Being skilled in fighting and showing no fear he quickly overcame his adversary, locked his head in a stranglehold and was about to kill him. At that moment the commoner, fighting for breath realized his fingers were touching the samurai's testicles. He gripped them hard and squeezed with all his might and in seconds the samurai was forced to release him and fell down in excruciating pain allowing his adversary to escape.

There are three aspects to Budo: *shin* (mind or spirit), *wasa* (technique) and *tai* (body). In Zen it is the same although some people focus only on mind and technique (zazen). Budo reminds us of the importance of the body. The body is the temple of the mind and without it no-one can practise either Budo or Zen. Taking care of our temple through correct nourishment and exercise is vital if we are to be able to maintain our practice. We must never forget or neglect the body for to do so makes us vulnerable to illness and harm. Without the body, the mind has no temple to be guardian of.

BUSHIDO:
THE WAY OF THE SAMURAI

The samurai were originally aristocratic warriors, not dissimilar to medieval knights, who emerged from provincial warrior bands and rose to power in Japan during the Kamakura period (1192–1333 CE) where they became political and social leaders. They continued to play a major role in Japanese government right up to the Meiji Restoration in 1868. During the Muromachi period (1338–1573 CE) they became very strongly influenced by Zen Buddhism and developed an unwritten code which held bravery, loyalty and honour above life itself. A samurai culture formed that influenced not only government and warfare, but also the arts and it was from this time that arts such as Chado (the Way of Tea) and Kado (the Way of Flower-arranging) emerged which are still practised today.

Bushido or the Way of the Warrior (*Bushi* – Warrior; *Do* – the Way) was the code of conduct for a samurai that held honour and duty above all else. The code varied in content during its historical development but throughout its use, the supreme obligation of a samurai was to his lord. It became strongly influenced by Confucian thought, stressing total obedience to authority even if obedience violated statute law. Honour and duty were held in such high regard that they even transcended life itself with ritual suicide by disembowelment (*seppuku*) becoming the only viable alternative for a samurai to dishonour or defeat. The samurai were noted for their strong martial spirit and fierceness in battle, but also for their frugal living, compassion and honesty.

At the onset of the Tokugawa period (1603–1867) the samurai became a closed caste and were forced by the ruling military dictatorship (*shogunate*) to take up non-military trades or become civil bureaucrats. As the Japanese merchant economy rose and urban culture developed, the position of the samurai declined. However, despite the decline of the samurai, in the mid-19th century, Bushido became the basis for the ethical training of the whole of Japanese society and the emperor replaced the feudal lord as the object of loyalty for all the samurai and society as a whole. It strongly influenced Japanese nationalism even beyond the decline of the samurai, right up until the end of the Second World War in 1945.

By the end of the Tokugawa period, many samurai families were suffering poverty and this led to the lower-ranking samurai joining a movement against the military regime that resulted in the Meiji Restoration of 1868. In 1871, feudalism in Japan came to an end, and the samurai lost their privileged

This armour was made for Yoshimura, the daimyo (feudal lord) of Sendai. The helmet dates from the 16th century and the armour from the mid-18th century.

position in society. During the 1870s, many discontented samurai rose up in rebellion. However, the newly established national army trained and supplied with modern weapons by the Americans swiftly suppressed these revolts. The story of this period in Japanese history is now famous through the film *The Last Samurai*.

This detail from the Heiji scroll depicts the samurai Minamoto Yoshitomo on horseback at the beginning of the Heiji insurrection of 1159.

THE SEVEN PRINCIPLES
OF BUSHIDO

Zen Buddhism strongly influenced Bushido thought, teaching such ideas as the pacification of the emotions, self-control in the face of all circumstances and the tranquil embracing of the inevitable. As Bushido developed it formed a set of seven principles that were regarded as essential for a samurai to follow religiously. These principles were practised to such a degree that they became the unconscious behaviour of the samurai even in the midst of the most violent and bloody confrontations on the battlefield.

The seven principles of Bushido are:

- *Gi*: right attitude, the truth

- *Yu*: bravery tinged with heroism

- *Jin*: unconditional love and compassion

- *Rei*: right action

- *Makoto*: complete sincerity and truthfulness

- *Melyo*: honour

- *Chugo*: devotion and loyalty.

These principles became the foundation of ethical teaching for all Japanese society and we can learn much from them in our own lives as we follow a path towards enlightenment. If we are seeking to uncover our own buddhanature, we can view these principles with the idea that our devotion and loyalty is set towards that inner buddhanature. The buddha within thus becomes our lord. If this is so, what do these principles have to teach us?

Gi

Gi is not only about the right attitude, but also about the realization of truth. The truth requires no belief; it stands on its own. When it is our time to die, it is our time to die. It also implies the idea of moral uprightness and integrity. Maintaining the right attitude and comprehending the innate truth of human nature helps us to break down delusions. To actively seek to understand the truth about what we are really like and who we are is vital if we are to break out of self-illusion and turn our weaknesses into strengths.

Yu

Yu, bravery tinged with heroism, may seem only to apply to warriors, but how can we ever hope to vanquish the ego if we do not have it? The ego is our greatest adversary and only the brave can ever hope to defeat it and realize enlightenment. It takes great courage to face your true Self, to recognize all your faults and weaknesses, and even more courage to let them go. The hero does not act selfishly, but becomes a hero by denying the Self and battling valiantly for his lord. So too must we battle valiantly for the Buddha within if we are to be victorious in our fight with the Self. When the ego is not mastered, bravery falls to mindless aggression.

Jin

Jin is without doubt the most important of all these principles for without love and compassion we are little more than savages. It is indeed noble to have love and compassion for those around us but this cannot be achieved if we do not first have love and compassion for ourselves. It is self-love that allows us to comprehend our weaknesses and view them compassionately rather than becoming lost in self-judgment. This love allows us to see and then release the humanness we carry so that we can realize our true buddhanature.

Rei

Rei not only implies right action but courteousness. Courteousness means being considerate and respectful in all manner and actions. If one wants to be free, one must respect the freedom of all others and this includes allowing and respecting other's views even if they directly contradict our own views.

Makoto

Makoto arises naturally from right action, for sincerity and truthfulness are acts of true respect. Besides if we tell lies to others, we are also lying to ourselves and this only occurs when we are attached to outcomes and desires. It is folly to imagine that friendship and popularity can be gained through lies. If we are always truthful, we will gain the respect of others and also feel at peace with ourselves. Telling lies causes stress and this in turn causes suffering.

Melyo

Melyo means honour, which in turn means the regard, respect and friendship shown to those worthy of receiving it. With regards to your Zen path, it is about realizing that you are worthy to seek and achieve buddhanature. It means having good self-esteem and not judging yourself.

After the Meiji Restoration of 1868 the samurai began to lose their privileged position in society. This photograph of a samurai court official was taken in the 1870s.

Chugo

Chugo is all about devotion and in the context of your Zen path it means remaining loyal and true to following your path no matter where it might take you and how it might unfold before you. There are times when we are deeply challenged and it is only through personal devotion and loyalty that we can hope to come through these challenges without losing our way.

JUDO

Judo (*Ju* meaning soft, supple, adaptable; *Do* meaning the way) is a Japanese martial art created and developed by Kano Jigoro (1860–1938) based on *jujitsu*, the gentle but powerful samurai art of unarmed combat that was created as a complement to the skills of swordsmanship. It utilizes techniques that use an opponent's force to one's own advantage rather than directly opposing it. One learns to adapt to an opponent's force and use softness to combat hardness; so the forward force of a punch will be taken and used in a gentle, combative throw.

Kano Jigoro studied jujitsu as a young man and changed from being a small, weak man into a highly respected master of unarmed combat.

Kano Jigoro was born on 28 October 1860 in the village of Mikage at a time of great political turbulence in Japan. Eight months prior to his birth, anti-shogunate activists assassinated the shogun great elder Naosuke Ii-tairo. This eventually led to the overthrow of the shogunate and the beginning of the Meiji Restoration (1867–68). In 1871, the feudal system collapsed and many samurai, including the masters of jujitsu, were forced to give up their old ways and seek new professions. In Tokyo, over one hundred jujitsu schools closed.

As a young man, Kano was greatly attracted to jujitsu, not least because he himself was of small frame and weak in constitution. He searched out the few remaining schools and one by one learned and mastered their various styles. In 1881 he graduated from Tokyo University and the following year founded the Kodokan School of Judo which initially had but one student, 17-year-old Tomita, who later reached the highest level of expertise in Judo, the tenth *dan* (grade). With few serious students, Kano financed his *dojo* (literally meaning the hall where the *do* is practised) through his work as a professor at Tokyo University and by translating books and documents for the ministry of education. In 1897 Lafcadio Hearn published a book in America introducing Judo and word of it began to spread through the Western world. In 1902, Kano sent one of his students, Yamashita, to the United States and Judo's place in the West was established.

The basis of Kodokan Judo is *Seiryoku Zenyo*, 'The Principle of the Best Use of Physical and Spiritual

Energy'. Kano emphasized that mastery in Judo could only be achieved through the cultivation of balance between body, mind and spirit. He taught many Zen principles in his school, especially those that lead to mastering the ego and emotions. He created five points that he felt constituted a well-balanced individual as follows:

- A person of good health

- A person of ethics and morals

- A person who is useful to the society they live in

- A person of strong will and courage

- A person who is diligent and hardworking.

A master of Judo utilizes his opponent's force and returns it to him in a gentle but firm manner. The results can be both powerful and dramatic.

One of the remarkable things about Kano was that throughout his life he was always popular and liked. Even after his death he was greatly loved by all who knew him. Perhaps part of his secret lies in his flexible and soft approach to life. It is very hard to dislike someone who offers no resistance to your thoughts, views and ideas, but who listens with humility and interest. Kano taught a skill that allowed one to transform a powerful enemy, without killing, domination or the use of any weapon, into a good friend.

DEVELOPING SOFTNESS AND FLEXIBILITY IN LIFE

Much of Kano's philosophy was based on the Taoist idea that one should be inwardly firm and strong while outwardly soft and supple. These ideas came from early texts such as the famous Sun Tsu classic of military strategy, *The Art of War* (500 BCE).

In this classic military text Sun Tsu states:

- One who is hard on the outside and strong on the inside will sooner or later be destroyed

- One who is soft on the outside and weak on the inside will eventually have everything taken from him

- One who is strong on the outside and weak on the inside will initially prosper but will eventually diminish

- One who is flexible on the outside and firm on the inside will continuously prosper.

From this we can see that being outwardly soft and flexible while inwardly firm and strong is the best path to happiness, health and freedom. In the West we are usually the opposite; we are firm on the outside arguing our views and correcting others when we think they are wrong, but ruled within by the emotions of regret, judgment, anger and desire. To be inwardly firm and strong means to not be swayed by the outside world with its chaos nor moved from our inner harmony by the actions of others. When life is challenging and especially when unexpected and extreme events occur in our lives, it is only by remaining true to ourselves, while adapting externally to the situation, that we can hope to navigate such occurrences with beauty and grace. This is the essence of Judo; to meet force with flexibility and persuasion with resoluteness.

Much of Taoist wisdom came from the observation of nature. The willow in the storm aptly shows the power of being externally flexible but internally firm.

Exercises for Developing Flexibility

One can find many practices that help to develop physical flexibility such as yoga, Tai Chi and martial arts, but the real skill in Judo is the development of mental flexibility. The following exercises are designed to help you let go of your ego and be more mentally flexible in your approach to life.

- When you are with people who say something that you perceive as wrong, either in pronunciation or meaning, do not correct them. Who are you to dictate how others should express themselves?

- When you visit someone's home and use his bathroom, leave it exactly as you found it. If the toilet seat is up when you arrive, leave it that way when you leave. If it is down, leave it that way when you leave. Stop exerting your preferences on other peoples' homes and other peoples' lives.

- When someone states an opinion that to you is wrong, search within your own mind for a perspective where what she says is right. The ability to 'bend your mind' to see other peoples' perspectives is a powerful tool in the understanding of others.

- When you find yourself making statements like 'It's a horrible, wet day today', see if you can find the opposite view, 'It's a wonderful, wet day today'. How do you know what a lovely sunny day is like if you cannot compare it to a wet day? Learn to appreciate the opposite to all your views.

AIKIDO

Aikido (*Ai* means coordinate; *Ki* means energy or spirit; *Do* means the way) is known as 'the way of spiritual harmony' and is unique among martial arts as it was developed without the employment of offensive moves. Ueshiba Morihei created it as a martial art in Japan after he had spent many years studying jujitsu in Tokyo. Ueshiba Morihei was born in 1883 in the small village of Tanabe. At the age of 15 he left his village and moved to Tokyo where he studied at various schools of the *do*. Although small in stature, he was robust and strong and quickly became a formidable martial artist.

Ueshiba's Aikido skills became well known and he attracted many students and challengers, but no one could defeat him. He taught Aikido without the use of words using action and the transmission of direct experience as his primary teaching method. His dojo was not unlike a monastery with training done in total silence. Ueshiba emphasized the development of *ki* and the mastery of the mind, teaching that one can only overcome an opponent if one is mentally calm and fully flexible. Students were taught the art of peace and defence, learning to subdue opponents and render their attacks harmless using the least possible effort and the simplest of physical techniques.

One day the famous Japanese boxer Horiguchi, nicknamed 'The Piston', visited Ueshiba's dojo and challenged the master to a match. Ueshiba consented and invited the boxer to attack him with full force. The boxer violently attacked the master reigning continuous and crushing blows to his chest. The master stood unmoved and then with lightning speed reached out and struck Horiguchi's arms from the outside. The boxer never had time to react and fell to the ground with both his arms broken. Even in his older years Ueshiba was a man of amazing skill and ability. At the age of 61, the Asahi News Journal made a film of him performing Aikido. 15 Judo practitioners surrounded him, each one attempted to pin him down, but he threw them all off with a single, miraculous movement.

Ueshiba was a truly remarkable man with an iron will, tremendous strength and yet a soft and flexible personality. In 1930, his student Mochizuki Minoru opened his own dojo at Shizuoka and invited the master to attend. Ueshiba arrived with a group of his young students and after the ceremony they all decided to climb the Nippon Daira plateau, an ascent of some five miles, to view the beautiful surrounding countryside. The master was wearing a traditional *hakama* (ceremonial dress) and *geta* (wooden clogs) and yet he climbed with such speed and agility that his students quickly got left behind. They attempted to take a short cut through some tea fields in order to catch up with the master. They took no heed of the fact that they were damaging crops and the nearby farmers, seeing their actions, ran towards them wielding bamboo staffs to drive them off.

The students, amused by the farmers' anger and half in jest took up positions as if to fight. At the moment the two opposing sides met they were stunned by the sudden appearance of Master Ueshiba. He had seen the situation and quickly retraced his steps. He stood before the farmers, knelt down and formally bowed to them saying, 'Please accept my formal and humble apology. Our actions are inexcusable and as you can see, I am at your disposal. These men are my young students; they were following me and lost their way because I climbed too quickly.' The farmers were amazed by this man's humility and themselves apologized for their hasty actions. Thus the master achieved a peaceful resolution without fighting.

As the master and students continued their climb, the students were all silent expecting a severe reprimand when they reached the summit. However when they arrived, Master Ueshiba smiled and said to them, 'the work of a farmer is very hard and tiring. They work long hours for very little money. Their job is never finished and their wages are never enough. The master and student of the *do*, on the other hand, work very little and are generally lazy. This is hardly just, is it? Ha, ha, ha...'

Many women are attracted to Aikido because of the grace and beauty of its techniques. This demonstration took place at the Forbidden City in Beijing.

KENDO

Kendo has its roots in the swordsmanship of the samurai warrior and unlike Judo and Aikido, does not have a single founder. It emerged in the late 18th century, when attitudes to combat were changing in Japan. In the comparative peace of the time, fighting skills were often only tested in duels. The *bokkun* (wooden sword) was introduced to minimize fatalities although they could still cause serious injury. Over several decades, various *ryu* (schools of martial arts) introduced further measures to reduce injury such as body armour and swords made of strips of flexible bamboo.

By the beginning of the Meiji Restoration, competitions had developed called *gekken* (conquering sword). Rules and equipment varied but the basis of competition was to make strikes at certain target areas designated by protective armour. In 1895 the rules became standardized and through further modifications in 1928 and 1948, Kendo as it is practised today was created.

Modern Kendo is divided into two practices; competitive training and *kata* (forms). Kata are prearranged moving forms that teach the fundamental skills and techniques of Kendo. They are performed in pairs and consist of seven long-sword forms and three short-sword forms. During training, great emphasis is placed on the *kamae* (posture). The correct posture in Kendo keeps the hips, trunk and head in line so that one can move in smooth and unbroken movements in any direction: forwards, backwards or sideways. In combative training cuts, parries and steps are taught using a *shinai* (four strips of bamboo with a hollow centre bound and tipped in leather).

In Kendo competitions, body armour is worn. It consists of a head and throat protector (called a *men*), a chest protector (*do*), wrist and hand protectors (*kote*) and a lower abdomen protector (*tare*). Target strikes are made to the centre and sides of the head, the right wrist, either side of the chest protector and a thrust to the throat protector. A cut will only score if it is made with a forward movement, is on target and accompanied by the correct step and shout. The shout is called a *kiai* (*ki* means spirit or energy; *ai* means meeting).

Great emphasis is also placed on the correct mental attitude and students of Kendo seek to achieve *zanshin*, a state of mind that is clear, calm and free of thought. This is the same mental clarity sought in zazen. The performance of rituals in the donning of armour and the preparation for combat are both designed to help teach this. Correct attitude, breathing, timing and foot positions are learned and practised in the kata until they arise naturally. In a Kendo encounter, a master will prepare for combat, attack, defend and conclude the fight while remaining inwardly still and calm. Kendo is both physically and mentally demanding and not for the faint-hearted. Although mainly practised by men in the West, those women who do take it up often do very well as they find it easy to develop a softness in their practice that can take men many years of devoted practice to achieve. In Kendo, the soft and flexible always wins over the hard and rigid.

'Why is the spirit or mind the most important?
Because in the end it is what decides.'

DESHIRMARU

Kendo developed in the late 18th century as a more peaceful way of maintaining and testing the skills and fighting techniques of the samurai swordsman.

OUTER AWARENESS, INNER CALM

In Kendo training great emphasis is placed on the eyes. The difference between victory and defeat can be attributed to where one looks and the manner in which one looks. Miyamoto Musashi, the famous Japanese swordsman and author of *The Book of Five Rings* taught that one should not be bothered by the outer appearance of an opponent, but rather one should look directly into his eyes in order to penetrate his mind. In this way one can see his inner intention before he knows it himself.

The eyes are the window to the soul and by looking into someone's eyes you can learn a great deal about them. The next time you are sitting with friends watching a film, take a few moments during the film to look at other people's eyes. If the film is gripping you will see them staring intensely, if it is sad you will see the emotion in their eyes, perhaps even a tear. So often our eyes betray how much our minds are taken by the things we observe. In conversations we use the eyes as a means of communication to show interest, disbelief, surprise and empathy. This is all perfectly natural but once you become aware of how you interpret what you see, you will find that often the mind takes what the eyes see and connects it with negative emotions. In this way the eyes can become the doorways to suffering.

'*If you don't understand the Way as it meets your eye, how can you know the Path as you walk it?*'

SHIH-T'OU

Practising Outer Awareness and Inner Calm

If we have no awareness of the power of vision to move us emotionally, we are prone to becoming victims of what we observe. In a crisis situation, many people will not act mindfully because what they see causes them shock and horror. It connects with their deepest fears and this fear clouds the mind. The following exercises will help you to be less inwardly moved by what you see and will thus enable you to cope better with the unexpected when it manifests into your life.

• On a fine day, go to your local park; sit on a bench and 'people-watch'. Observe all that is going on but do not let your mind be taken by anything. See the happiness and sadness of children playing, watch it and let it go. Observe the way people walk, noting whether they walk hurriedly or calmly, but make no judgments about them. Look at the trees, the sky and everything around you but keep your expression the same no matter what you observe. As you walk home try to keep your eyes open and mind alert, but calm.

• Many people like watching soaps on television. They often become addicted to them because their minds become taken by the fictional drama that is unfolding before them. They feel elated when the characters are happy and morbidly fascinated when the story line depicts tragedy or conflict. The next time you have an opportunity to watch a soap, try to do so without being emotionally taken by the events. Remember it is just a story and try to look at it in a deeper, less emotionally driven way. Look beyond the story at the camera work, the scenery, the acting and music. Observe everything and yet be taken by nothing.

• The next time you are a passenger on a train, open your eyes and awareness to everything that is going on around you. Do not get lost in imagination but stay totally present in the moment. Observe the changes that occur as you travel both outside of the carriage and inside. Try to view everything without judgment. If you see beautiful countryside, say to yourself, 'How wonderful,' if you see wasteland filled with weeds and litter, say to yourself, 'How wonderful.' Your appreciation of everything and everyone you see should be the same. Nothing is better or worse, more pleasant or unpleasant. There is beauty in everything and everyone if you just open your eyes and awareness to see it.

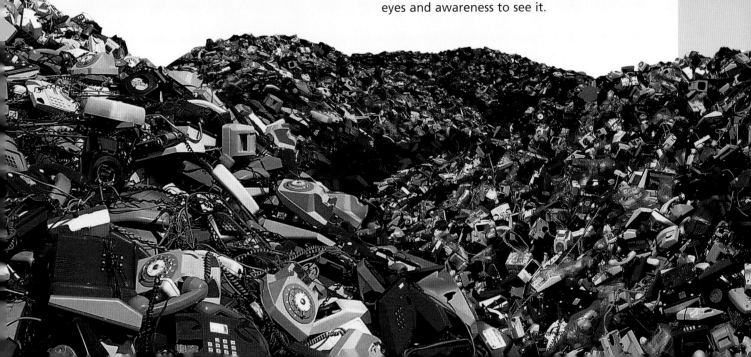

KYUDO

Kyudo, 'the way of the bow' is perhaps the most esoteric of the Japanese martial arts and the true mastery of it takes the devotion of a lifetime. Unlike Kendo, it is less of a sport, but more a form of moving meditation. In Kyudo, the hitting of the target is secondary to the state of mind of the archer. Through mental training the archer learns not only to be one with his bow, but also one with the target.

The first written reference to archery in Japan dates back to the 3rd century CE and tells of the pregnant Empress Jingo binding her body with bowstrings in order to ensure that her son would be a strong and fit warrior. The Japanese bow became a formidable weapon of warfare for the samurai and was noted for its length and power. In the 12th century, Tamatono, a leading samurai, had a bow that was nearly 3 m (10 ft) long and took the strength of three men to string it. In one battle he fired an arrow at an enemy and the force of the shot was so great that the arrow passed clean through its target and killed another man behind. Tamatono was eventually captured and his captors severed the tendons in his arm to prevent him ever using a bow again. As a result Tamatono committed the first recorded act of *seppuku* (ritual suicide).

From the beginning of the Tokugawa period the 'way of the bow' emerged, with the emphasis being not on hitting the target, but on achieving a mental state of pure awareness and emptiness with no ambition to succeed or fail. The practice of shooting became more ritualized and it is this form that exists today. Kyudo nearly died out at the beginning of the 20th century but achieved a great revival in 1923 and today is practised by more than half a million people in Japan and throughout the Western world.

To achieve perfection in Kyudo takes many years of training the mind and body so that they act together in perfect unison. Body, mind, bow and arrow all become one.

Kyudo Breathing Exercise

The Chozen-ji school of Kyudo teaches breathing exercises combined with simple movements as part of a student's training. What follows is a simple exercise that originates in China as part of the Ba Duan Jin – the eight fine exercises that were taught to Zen monks to improve their health and wellbeing. It is called 'Shooting the Bow'.

1 Stand with your feet parallel, a shoulder's width apart. While breathing in through the nose, bend the knees a little and raise your hands in front of your chest, palms facing inwards as if you were holding a large beach ball.

2 Lower your left elbow and turn your left hand so that your hand is facing away to your left side with your fingers pointing up. At the same time turn your head to face left and slightly bend the fingers of your right hand as if holding a bowstring.

3 Breathe out as you extend your left hand out to the left while at the same time drawing your right elbow back slightly as if pulling on the bow string. Hold this stretch for a second before relaxing.

4 Breathe in as you return your hands to in front of your chest as if your were again holding a large beach ball.

5 Repeat stages 2–4 on the right side of the body.

6 Continue to the left side and then to the right side again performing the exercise four times on each side.

The Eight Stages of Kyudo

'Having drawn sufficient,
No longer pull, but keep it
still without holding,
The bow should never know
When the arrow is to fly.'

TRADITIONAL KYUDO POEM

The act of preparing to shoot, drawing the bow and releasing the arrow in Kyudo is divided into eight stages. Each stage is performed in a calm and mindful way, being fully present in the moment and free of intention. A sequence of actions is performed prior to these eight stages, while sitting, to prepare body, mind and spirit.

- *Ashibumi*: Setting the feet and legs in the correct place

- *Dozukuri*: Aligning the head and trunk and preparing to use the bow

- *Yugamae*: Placing the arrow notch into the bowstring

- *Uchiokoshi*: Raising the bow and looking towards the target

- *Hikiwake*: Drawing the bow using the unique Mongolian lock where the thumb holds the bow string

- *Kai*: Preparation of body and mind to release the arrow

- *Hanare*: The release of the arrow

- *Zazshin*: A state of total awareness where the archer listens to the bowstring. A Kyudo master can tell if his shot has been successful just by listening to the sound of the string.

In Kyudo the archer seeks to become one with the bow and the target. Every deliberate action is a step closer to that oneness.

SHODO – JAPANESE CALLIGRAPHY

'Your highest objective is to become one with the vibrant
rhythm of nature and to let this pulsation flow out
through the brush.'

FROM *BRUSH MEDITATION* BY H.E. DAVEY

THE WAY OF CALLIGRAPHY

Calligraphy has been in use for thousands of years and in the West it developed into styles that are noted for their uniformity. In the Orient, however, calligraphy has developed into an art form which celebrates the individuality of the artist and the uniqueness of the moment in which the art is created. Most modern languages use phonetic symbols to create words, whereas the languages of Chinese and Japanese are based on ideographs, where each written word is actually a picture representation of the object it describes. There are about two hundred basic ideographs from which some forty thousand characters can be written.

This 20th-century piece of calligraphy was created by a monk from the Daitoku-Ji monastery, Kyoto, Japan.

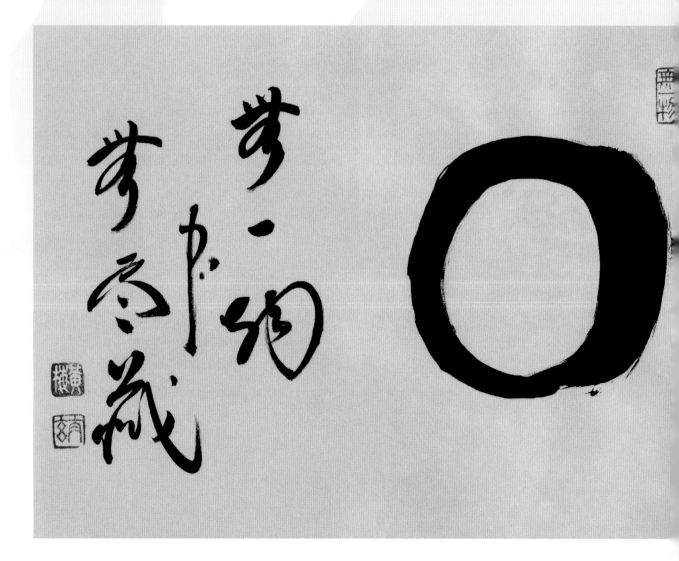

Shodo (*Sho* means 'brush writing' and *Do* means 'the way') is an art form that in Japan rivals poetry and painting in its importance. The art is instant with characters often taking only a few seconds to create, but one should not be fooled into thinking that this makes Shodo easy to learn. Characters cannot be changed once written; there is no touching up or altering, just the expression of the moment however perfect or imperfect that moment might seem. Writing is done with a simple, supple brush dipped in ground ink to form strokes of varying character and rhythmic execution.

In forming these letters, a master of Shodo can create infinite variations balancing the flow of the brush with the tension in the wrist, and the calmness of the mind with the intent behind each word. The brush is not merely a tool used for writing, but becomes an extension of the writer; a means through which the writer shows his individuality and personality as he writes in an expression of his deep inner consciousness. Just as in the samurai tradition there is unity between body, mind and sword; so in Shodo there is unity between body, mind and brush. Mastery of this art takes many years of practice and formal instruction and often in Japan it is taught from a very early age. Today in Japan it is still studied by a large proportion of the population from young to old and housewives to business executives.

Intrinsically linked to Zen throughout its history, many of the greatest Shodo masters of the past have also been masters of Zen. Perhaps the most famous is a Buddhist monk named Kukai. One story tells of how the Emperor Tokusoketui asked him to rewrite a five-column section of a panelled screen that had become damaged over time. Kukai took hold of five brushes, one in each hand, one gripped between the toes of each foot and one held between his teeth and immediately re-wrote the five columns simultaneously!

The letters in Japanese calligraphy are formed using a brush called a *fude* dipped in ink traditionally made from the soot of burned oil or wood combined with fishbone or hide glue. In traditional Chinese calligraphy all letters are created with single strokes drawn in a specific order, however in Japan two faster (but less legible) styles of writing have developed called *Gyosho* (semicursive) and *Sosho* (cursive) which can be seen as similar to the joined-up style of writing Roman letters.

Calligraphy and painting are often combined in Shodo as in this mural by the Japanese artist Miyakawa Choshun using ink on rice paper.

THE HISTORY OF CALLIGRAPHY IN THE ORIENT

Oriental calligraphy originated in China around 2700 BCE as carvings on tortoiseshell and bone and later was used for religious purposes such as inscribing bells. During the Ch'in dynasty (221–206 BCE) the various styles that had emerged were synthesized into a uniform style called *Tensho* or seal script. Tensho is the most formal style of writing with characters showing left and right symmetry and being well balanced in both horizontal and vertical planes. It is still used today in China for official certificates and seals. It was also during the Ch'in dynasty that the use of inks, brushes and silk first arose.

During the Han and Six dynasties periods (206 BCE–589 CE), several new writing styles emerged. The first was *Reisho*, clerical script, which is similar in style to seal script except that the left-right symmetry is no longer as apparent and the script tends to be more horizontal and flatter. The other three main styles were *Sosho* or cursive script which was more flowing, *Kaisho* or standard script with printed-style characters usually in the form of a square and *Gyosho* or semicursive script.

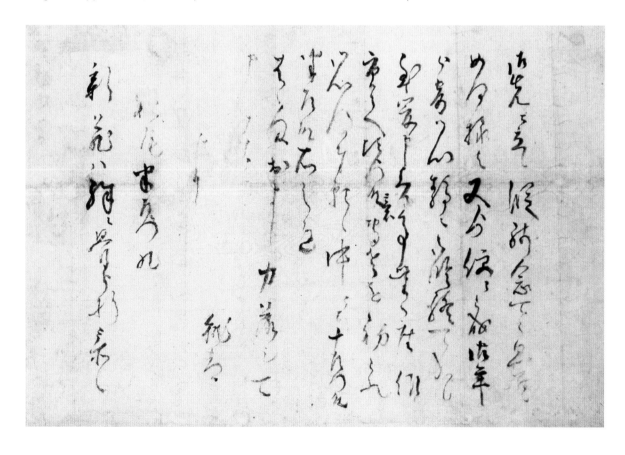

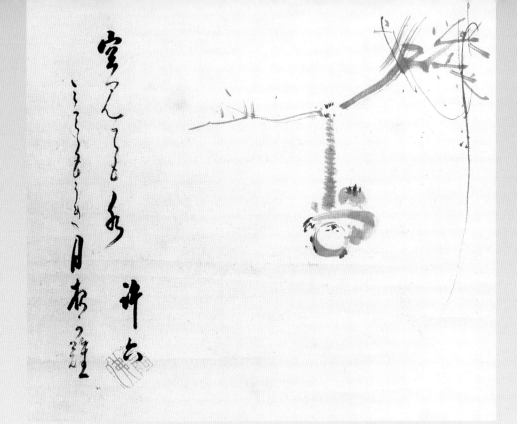

This calligraphy was created by Matsuo Basho with the painting by one of his disciples.

Calligraphy arrived in Japan during the 6th century along with Buddhism and by this time all five of the main styles of Chinese calligraphy had already been well established. Early exponents of Shodo included the Buddhist monk Kukai (774–835 CE), the emperor Saga (786–842 CE) and a courtier named Tachibana Hayanari (died 842). In the 10th century Michikaze (894–966 CE) created a new, dignified style that was further modified by Fujiwara Yukinari (972–1028 CE) and Shodo became established as a national art form in Japan. By this time a phonetic Japanese alphabet had become established in which Chinese characters represented a syllable and were called *kana* characters. Three types of kana emerged namely *mayogana*, *hiragana* and *katakana*. It was also during this period that a 31-syllable style of Japanese poetry called *waka* became very popular and it became fashionable to write these poems down on beautifully decorated sheets of paper.

From the 10th century, the women of the Japanese Imperial Court wrote prose in the form of essays, histories, fiction and diaries. One of the most famous authoresses of this time was Murasaki

This poem by arguably the greatest Japanese haiku poet Matsuo Basho, was written two days before his death. In it he apologizes to his disciples for dying before them.

Shikibu (c.978–1014 CE), who was prolific and diverse in her prose. Her most famous work is a novel entitled *Genji monogatari* (*The Tale of Genji*) that has fifty-four chapters. The kana style was well suited for the lengthy prose created by the women of the time and so also became known as *onnamoji* ('female letters'). In the 17th century, the famous poet Matsuo Basho (1644–1694), who was born as a samurai but lived life as a monk, created beautiful calligraphy of his *haiku* poems.

Today Shodo is a hugely popular throughout Japan and is continually increasing in popularity worldwide, especially with the spread of Zen. Its approach and philosophy is intrinsically linked to Zen thought as shown in the traditional Shodo proverb that states: 'If your mind is correct, the brush will be correct'. Not only is this art form a spiritual practice, but it also gives a deep insight into the nature of the artist for one who can 'read between the lines'. It is even said that the health of a Shodo disciple can be seen through his art with defects showing in his work as *byohitsu* ('sick strokes'). Because Shodo is an art form, one does not need to understand the meaning of the characters to appreciate its vibrant beauty. Each work is unique and evocative and the more you look at the beauty within its simplicity, the more you see of the true nature of Zen.

PICTURES IN WORDS

In the English language, as in most other languages, we have a limited number of symbols that are combined to represent words, the 26 letters of the alphabet. In Chinese and Japanese, however, pictographs are used to represent words and concepts and there are literally thousands of symbols used in their languages. Sometimes a single symbol is used to represent a word but more often a combination of symbols are used to expand the meaning of the word and give it a more conceptual meaning.

mountain (old)   **mountain (new)**   **yin**   **yang**

An example of a single symbol used to represent a word is the sign for 'mountain'. Here we can plainly see that the symbol shows three peaks and is derived from the ancient pictogram for mountain.

One of the most famous concepts of oriental philosophy is that of yin and yang. Yin and yang are complimentary opposites and are used in Zen to teach balance and the middle way. Yang represents light, sun, activity and masculine while yin represents darkness, moon, rest and feminine. The original meaning of yin and yang is the dark and sunny side of a hill as can be seen in the characters as follows:

mound   **cloud**   **sun**   **sun over**   **rays of**
or hill   **the**   **light**
                                             horizon

左右

left   **right**

Likewise the characters for 'left' and 'right' imply this yin/yang balance as the character for left includes the symbol for work (yang) while the character for right includes the symbol for mouth (yin), the latter representing the need to eat in order to work.

Many of the combined pictograms used in Japanese and Chinese also give an insight into the philosophy of the orient. For example, the symbol for peace is the combination of two pictograms, one representing the mouth, the other brown rice, thus implying that if you want peace, keep the people fed. Indeed, one of the biggest causes for war in the past had been the desire of a nation to acquire land so that it could better feed its people.

work   **mouth**

氣

chi

One of the most difficult concepts to translate in oriental philosophy is that of Chi (Japanese 'Ki'). It is variously translated as 'energy', 'spirit', 'essence', 'life-force' and 'vitality'. However a study of the character for Chi shows us that it is made up of two symbols. At the bottom of the character is the symbol for uncooked brown rice and above it is the symbol for 'steam'. This would imply that if you want to understand the concept of Chi, all you need do is cook brown rice. Perhaps this is why rice is such an integral part of most Zen disciples' diets.

vapour,   **(uncooked)**
steam,   **rice**
gas

WRITING AS MEDITATION

The practice of Shodo inevitably leads into two further Zen paths, Gado (the 'Way of Painting') and Kado (the 'Way of Poetry'). Zen masters have used poetry in their teachings since earliest times to demonstrate enlightenment.

The best-known style of Zen poetry is the haiku. Haiku is traditionally a poem of three lines of five, seven and five syllables, usually containing a seasonal reference and a spiritual statement. It is practised as a meditative art by the Tenro School of Zen. Students often meet to compose as many as one hundred haiku, from which perhaps one will be chosen and further worked on for months until it is deemed to be finished. The Soun ('free verse') school of Zen poetry does not adhere to the 17-syllable rule and instead composes short and compact verses in the spirit of Basho (1644–1694), one of the greatest ever Zen poets.

Writing a haiku appears simple but writing a good Zen haiku can take years of practice. The special quality of great haiku requires you to be fully in the moment so that you can paint a picture in words. One of Basho's most famous haiku is:

Leap-splash – a frog.

Another is:

Year's end –
Still in straw hat
And sandals.

To write a great haiku, you cultivate oneness with all you observe. To begin, you focus your mind on an object, such as an empty bowl. Initially, your mind will conjure up images that describe the bowl or its contents, such as air, water, hands, stillness, apples. You then let these thoughts go, recognizing them as mere perceptions or mental illusions. You continue to focus on the bowl until such thoughts stop arising. Instead of looking at the bowl, you become one with the bowl and begin perceiving as the bowl. This state of oneness is called *muga*. Your oneness with the bowl silences your mind's erratic chatter and allows your ego to disappear. The perceptions that arise in this state are the basis for your haiku.

A simple way for you to begin to understand this process is to find a bridge over a stream. Stand on it, looking down at the running water. Initially you will perceive yourself and the bridge as still, with the water running beneath you. Keep observing the stream until it becomes still, and it is the bridge and you that move instead!

Haiku Meditation

YOU WILL NEED
- Pen
- Paper

1 Find a natural place, for instance a park or garden, and sit down in a cross-legged position and relax.

2 Start by observing the breath as it travels in and out of your nostrils. When you feel still and relaxed, go on to the next step.

3 Close your eyes and begin counting your breaths as follows: In (one), out (two), in (three), out (four), and so on up to ten.

4 If you lose count or your mind begins to wander, begin again at one and count until you reach ten.

5 When you reach number ten open your eyes and other senses and observe your first impressions. Do not let your mind enquire. Just observe the moment.

6 Write down these first impressions as simply as possible, without thinking about them. For instance, wind on face, breathe, dancing pines.

7 Sit quietly and read the words you have written while recalling all the feelings that your first impression evoked.

8 Close your eyes again and think only about the moment you have just experienced.

9 Make a note of any deeper impressions that this meditation has evoked.

10 Use the notes you have made to write three lines, using short and simple words that capture your perceptions and any deeper impressions.

FUNDAMENTALS OF SHODO

When writing Japanese calligraphy, attention is placed upon the Zen concepts of simplicity, inner calm, correct posture and breathing. Letters are written effortlessly, allowing the brush to flow naturally across the parchment. Each written piece not only expresses the meaning of the words, but also the state of mind of the writer and the 'flavour' of the words. Just as a Japanese winter flower arrangement may evoke feelings of warm sun on a frosty morning, so too the writing of a simple poem about nature will evoke much more than the mere meaning of the words.

A piece of Japanese calligraphy will show balance between the letters and the overall composition and is imbued with dynamic rhythm. Straight lines are drawn strong and clear while curved lines show delicacy and mobility. Variance in the thickness or thinness of lines gives the piece a sense of flow and movement while consistency is shown by the amount of ink (or lack of it) used throughout the work. A Shodo master is like a fine musician. The letters are his score, the brush his instrument and through thoughtful interpretation, something unique and wonderful is created.

A Shodo Calligraphy Tool Set

The unique styles of Japanese calligraphy cannot be created without the use of certain tools and any serious student of Shodo will have their own set of tools kept in a special box called a *suzuribako*. A typical set of Shodo tools is as follows:

- *Shitajiki*: A soft, black mat used to provide a comfortable writing surface

- *Bunchin*: A metal stick used as a paperweight to hold the paper in place during writing

- *Hanshi*: Special, thin calligraphy paper

- *Futofude*: A thick brush used for writing the main characters

- *Hosofude*: A thin brush used for writing the artist's name and sometimes for other characters too

- *Suzuri*: A heavy, black inkstone

- *Sumi*: Solid black ink mixed with water in a suzuri to provide the writing medium. (Instant inks are also used these days)

- *Suiteki*: A dropper used to mix water with sumi.

This is a typical Japanese calligraphy set showing the brushes, inkstone, paperweight and other utensils in their special box called a suzuribako.

This painting by Yashima Gakutei (c.1786–1868) of the poetess Bijin shows her at her calligraphy table with all her writing equipment in place before her.

EXPERIENCING SHODO

One of the first characters a Shodo student learns to create is called the *enso*. It is not actually a proper character, but rather a piece of simple art that conveys great depth of meaning to a follower of Zen.

At first glance the enso is nothing more than a circle, but when executed correctly, it is a dynamic representation of the circle of infinity showing the balance of yin and yang and the vibrant movement of creation. It begins in stillness, transforms itself into dramatic motion and flows effortlessly towards completion with the energy at the end of the movement continuing off the page and into infinity. It begins in nothingness, ends in nothingness and represents nothingness.

When practising Shodo, one must be totally present in the moment with clear-minded concentration as seen in this Zen Master.

The Enso

YOU WILL NEED
- Brush
- Ink
- Paper

Ideally one should use a proper brush, ink and paper although for this exercise you can as easily use a thick-handled artist's brush, some Indian ink and drawing paper.

1 Sit in an upright position, ideally at a table with a straight-backed chair with a piece of paper firmly weighted down in front of you. Place your inkpot to the right hand side of the paper.

2 Take hold of the brush, about halfway up, between the thumb and the first two fingers, as if holding a pencil.

3 Before you begin take a few deep breaths in and out through your nose to calm your mind and body.

4 Dip the brush into the ink remembering that you will do this only once.

5 To begin the enso, press the brush firmly down on the left hand side of the paper.

6 Turn your wrist and arm in a smooth arc from left to right to form the circle decreasing the pressure continuously until the circle is complete.

7 The movement should be smooth and spontaneous with both mind and breath calm throughout. The hand must not stop abruptly but continue to flow even when the brush leaves the page.

8 You can repeat this exercise many times and learn something new about your Self each time you do so.

9 Do not be fooled by the simplicity of this exercise, it can teach you many things over many, many years.

KADO – THE ART OF FLOWER-ARRANGING

'Ikebana (Kado) does not exist independently by itself, but as a link in the whole universe, each part of which is endlessly connected with another.'

SENDENSHO

THE WAY OF FLOWERS

Kado, the way of flower-arranging, is more generally known today as *ikebana* (literally 'living flowers'). It began in Japan in the 6th century, has an extensive written history dating back to 1462 and was largely unknown in the West before the 1900s. In early days it was the provenance of Japanese royalty and the samurai with teachings and knowledge being passed exclusively through the monks of the major Buddhist temples in Japan.

For many hundreds of years Kado was not available to the ordinary Japanese folk but in recent times its teachings have become more accessible. Today it has grown into a worldwide art form equal to painting, sculpture and ceramics. Its principles are simple: to understand and express the feeling of the materials and to create an asymmetrical, three-dimensional display.

One of the major modern schools that has helped to spread the teachings of Ikebana worldwide is the Sogetsu School founded by Sofu Teshigahara in 1927. Sofu was part of a new movement that respected the traditional principles but brought new forms and materials into use. In 1933 he held his first solo exhibition at the Josui Kaikan in Tokyo including displays incorporating scrap metal. After the Second World War his displays utilized other materials including plastic and feathers and his 1949 exhibition at the Mitsukoshi Department Store revolutionized thinking and brought the art into the 20th century. His fundamental teaching was, 'the principles remain the same, the form is always changing.'

The Sogetsu School has gained worldwide respect and has moved and developed to mirror the great changes that have taken place in the world of Modern Art over the past 60 years. Indeed Sofu, its founder, was strongly influenced by such artists as Picasso and Dali. The school can boast many famous people who have both visited and attended lessons there, including Queen Elizabeth II, Princess Diana and Mrs Gandhi.

'Ikebana is not a mere decoration, it is an art. Ikebana is not for Japan alone, it is for the whole world.'

SOFU TESHIGAHARA

A Kado arrangement creates a particularly striking impression when placed in a simple, uncluttered setting.

THE HISTORY OF KADO

Shotoku Taishi (574–622) was the second son of the short-reigning Emperor Yomei. After a political upheaval, his aunt came to the throne and in 593 he became the crown prince and regent, a position he held until his death. Shotoku was a fervent Buddhist, great scholar and social and political reformer who instigated the opening of cultural, economic and political exchange with China.

In the early 7th century Taishi sent Ono no Imoko to China as an ambassador, where he learned about making offerings of flowers at Buddhist temples. He brought these ideas back to Japan and established the founding principle of Kado, which is that the arrangement consists of three parts, representing heaven, man and earth. He also taught the importance of harmony between man and nature, the second founding principle.

Ono no Imoko adopted the name of Senmo and when he ultimately became guardian of a temple in Kyoto, he devoted the rest of his life to making and offering simple, three-flower arrangements. He lived in a simple dwelling called *Ikenobo* (meaning 'the hut beside the pool') and it is from here that the oldest school of Kado, Ikebono, derived its name. One of his descendants, Senkei (died 1028) established the fundamental rules and principles of the Ikebono School that are still followed today. He introduced the *Rikka* style (meaning 'standing flowers'), creating enormous floral displays, often the height of a man, to represent the mythical Mount Meru of Buddhist cosmology. By the 16th century,

Sofu Teshigahara was influential in bringing Ikebana into the realm of modern art.

Kado was well established as an art form in Japan with many rules and theories. The Japanese aristocracy undertook training in Kado and even the military ruler of Japan at the time took lessons from the famous aesthetician Sen Rikyu. It is Sen Rikyu who is said to have been the first to

Huon Ohara resurrected the shallow bowl arrangements used in the moribana style.

create an arrangement in the *Nageire* style (meaning 'to throw in') when a student asked him to demonstrate his skill and imagination with some irises blooming in his garden. Sen Rikyu nonchalantly cut a few stems and threw them into a wooden bucket, creating a stunning masterpiece. This casual and less formal approach grew in popularity as an alternative to the complex rigours of the Rikka style.

In the 18th century the *Seika* style (sometimes called 'Shoka style') was established by combining the rules of Rikka with the free expression of Nageire. Its main idea was that an arrangement should consist of three branches rising from a single source with each branch forming a graceful curve toward heaven. At the beginning of the 20th century, with the introduction of European flowers to Japan, new trends in Kado became established. In 1910, a sculptor and Kado master named Unshin Ohara formed a school based on one of the original, but neglected styles of Kado, shallow bowl arrangements. His *Moribana* style (meaning 'heaped-up flowers') quickly gained popularity and many of his disciples went on to form their own schools of Kado. This further led to 'free-style' arrangements, called *jiyubana*.

In 1930 a group of art critics and flower masters established a new style called *Zen'ei Ikebana* (avant-garde flowers) drawing up a manifesto declaring that all rules and theories of the past be rejected. Among this group was Ikenobo master Sofu Teshigahara (1900–79) who founded the Sogetsu School in 1927. He was the first to discover the beauty of dead branches and withered leaves and went on to introduce elements such as bits of iron, brass and stone into his arrangements. This later evolved into the utilization of all sorts of non-plant materials such as metals, vinyl, plastic and feathers into Kado.

Today there are several thousand schools of Kado in Japan varying in size, some with thousands and others with millions of adherents. Each school has its own rules of arrangement and variation in style but broadly fall into three categories: Ikenobo, Ohara or Sogetsu style. In 1956, Ellen Gordan Allen, wife of an American general, who had studied and graduated from the Ohara School, established 'Ikebana International' to promote the study of Kado throughout the world. It is largely through her enthusiasm that since 1959 the heads of the principal schools in Tokyo have regularly toured the world giving demonstrations and lectures as well as allowing Western study groups to come and train in Japan. Kado, or Ikebana, is now a worldwide art form and its popularity continues to grow.

This display is typical of the style of the Sogetsu School of Ikebana.

THE DIFFERENT STYLES OF KADO

Over the centuries, five main styles of Kado have developed namely Rikka, Nageire, Seika/Shoka, Moribana and Zen'ei Ikebana. Each style has its own set of rules and underlying principles.

Seika/Shoka

The Seika arrangements stress naturalness and simplicity. They are usually triangular in shape based on three primary lines: *shin*, the central line of 'truth', *soe*, the supporting branches, and *tai*, branches placed at the base to provide balance. The whole arrangement symbolizes the universe made up of three parts: heaven, man and earth. All designs follow the natural order of creation with plants native to the mountain regions being used for the tallest parts and lowland plants for the base. Plants are placed in an upright position to mimic their natural growth pattern and special attention is taken to create a natural display with all elements harmonized to the season.

Moribana

The Moribana style creates naturalistic landscapes in a flat tray, box or dish. The stems are held in place by insertion into a needlepoint holder called a *kenzan*. Unlike its more traditional predecessors, it sometimes uses imported Western flowers. It has a three-dimensional approach creating the arrangement in terms of foreground, middle ground and distance. The dish is divided into four quarters as follows: the quarter facing the room represents the south and summer;

The moribana style (meaning 'heaped-up flowers') was created by Huon Ohara and was based on an old neglected style of Kado.

the one farthest away the north and winter; to the right is the east and spring; to the left is the west and autumn. The arrangement is placed in the quarter corresponding to the season with the other three quarters holding water.

Rikka

Rikka arrangements were originally seven-branched arrangements to symbolize the mythical Mount Meru: the branches represented its peak (*ryo*), waterfall (*ro*), hill (*qaku*), the valley behind (*bi*) and the town in front (*shi*) with the whole piece divided into *in* (shade or yin) and *yo* (sun or yang). The three main branches of *shin* ('Truth'), *soe* ('supporting') and *nagashi* ('flowing') are suggestive of a high mountain, a distant mountain and a near road

respectively and are placed so that their tips form a scalene triangle (a triangle with three unequal sides). Rikka later developed a nine-branched and then eleven-branched style. Huge arrangements up to 5 m (16 ft) high were sometimes created using, for example, white holly blossoms to represent snow-capped mountains and cascades of white chrysanthemums to symbolize waterfalls.

Nageire

The traditional principles of Kado emphasize triangular structure and harmonious colours, but the nageire style looks more towards spontaneity and freshness. Nageire originally denoted all flower arrangements that were not of the rikka style. Later in the 17th century it applied to the lavish and large arrangements that were popular at the time. Today it refers to simple, yet flexible designs that reflect the highly changeable times we live in. It is most often expressed as a simple arrangement placed in a tall upright vase with the flowers placed together in either the right or left front quarter of the vase.

Zen'ei Ikebana

The Zen'ei Ikebana style (avant-garde) of flower arranging broke all the established traditions when it rose to fame in the 1930s. Stems were crossed instead of being kept distinct and separate, even numbers of stems were used as opposed to the traditional odd numbers, and leaves were cut to form artificial shapes. Paint was sometimes applied to arrangements, supporting wires were made visible rather than hidden, and unorthodox modern materials such as plastic and glass were included. Zen'ei Ikebana has revolutionized kado and brought it up to date with the modern, changing times, although many millions of exponents still favour the more traditional styles.

The Nageire style (meaning 'to throw in') was thought to have been first created by the famous Kado master Sen Rikyu.

THE FUNDAMENTALS OF KADO

Most basic Kado arrangements work on the principle of three main parts using three stems of different lengths, although sometimes only two stems are used and on rare occasions only one. The three stems from tallest to shortest are called *shin*, *soe* and *tai* (or *hikae*) but for ease of understanding we will label them A, B and C respectively. All three stems must complement each other in shape, colour, line and mood being either similar or contrasting. A (*shin*), being the tallest, sets the overall character of the arrangement; B (*soe*) complements and supports A; C (*tai*) provides balance to the two taller stems and completes the arrangement.

The Moribana style is noted for its naturalistic displays.

Generally either A and B or B and C use plants of the same kind although on occasions all three stems come from the same plant and on others three different plant stems are used. However, the use of three different plants presents a major challenge to achieve a natural but ordered arrangement. So that the arrangement shows vitality and mimics the natural variation created in nature, stems are placed at different angles as well as heights. This creates a truly three-dimensional arrangement that can be viewed from a variety of angles.

To create visual effect, stems are often bent and this is achieved by making the stem wet and with wet hands gently applying pressure above and below the point of bend. Tougher stems are sometimes twisted slightly to gently break some of the plant fibres and allow bending while thick stems are cut about a third of the way through and then bent. A variety of techniques is also used to hold stems in place. Light branches are cut at the base so that the angle of the cut corresponds to the angle of the side of the vase. Bigger branches are supported by attaching a small horizontal stick halfway up the stem or at the base,

inserting it into a split. Beginners can also use wire although experts in Kado pride themselves on producing stunning arrangements with the minimum use of support.

The three main stems are cut to heights that correspond to the size of the vase using prescribed formulas. Each school has its own formula based on the height and width of the vase. In the Ikebono School, for example, stem A is one and a half times the width plus the height. Stem B is three quarters the height of A and stem C half the height of A. So if the vase were 6 cm (2⅓ in) wide and 12 cm (4½ in) high, stem A would measure 21 cm (8¼ inches) ([one and a half times six] plus twelve), stem B would measure 15.75 cm (6⅛ in) (twenty-one times three quarters), and stem C would measure 10.5 cm (4 in) (twenty-one divided by two).

These are the basic rules that will help to ensure the arrangement achieves balanced proportion and line, although all schools teach that sometimes one has to dispense with the rules if the occasion demands. In Zen, sometimes you have to forget what you know to discover a deeper knowledge.

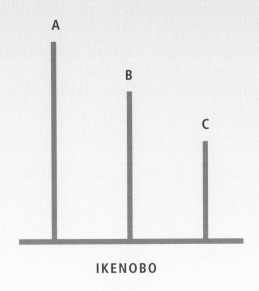

IKENOBO

A = (1.5 x width of vase) + height of vase
B = height of A x 0.75
C = height of A x 0.50

MAKING A KADO ARRANGEMENT

A basic Nageire arrangement uses three stems and a tall, deep vase. The nature of the vase lends itself to stately, tall displays so the length of the stems is as follows: The tallest stem (A) is two times the height plus the width of the opening of the vase. The second stem (B) is three-quarters the height of A and the shortest stem (C) is half the height of A. The usual height of the vase is 15–25 cm (6–10 in) although a vase as small as 7cm (2¾ in) may be used for miniature arrangements. The name Nageire means 'to throw in' and so this kind of arrangement must look spontaneous whilst retaining line, form and balance. Nageire arrangements occupy the front left or right quarter of the vase.

Making a Simple Nageire Arrangement

YOU WILL NEED
- A tall, deep vase
- Two tall leafy stems and a shorter flower stem
- A pair of clippers or scissors
- Supporting aids such as sticks, string or wire

4 Cut the flowering stem to half the height of the tallest stem.

5 Place the tallest stem in the vase first, bending it slightly if necessary to create a gently flowing line. Place it towards the back of the front left or right quarter of the vase.

1 Measure the height and width of the opening of the vase.

2 Cut the tallest stem to an approximate length (twice the height of the vase plus the width of the vase.)

3 Cut the next tallest stem to three quarters the height of the first stem.

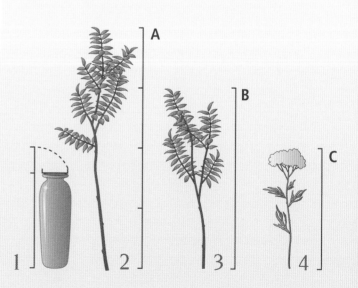

This Nageire arrangement in a tall upright vase uses a slanting style to create extra width and a sense of movement in the display.

6 Cut the base of stem B at an angle so that when placed in the vase, it makes a 45-degree angle with the ground. Place this stem in front of stem A.

7 Bend stem C in the opposite direction to stem A so it forms a line that is only 15 to 30 degrees to the ground. Place C in front of the other two stems on the opposite side to A. Gently adjust the flowers until they look and feel in the correct positions.

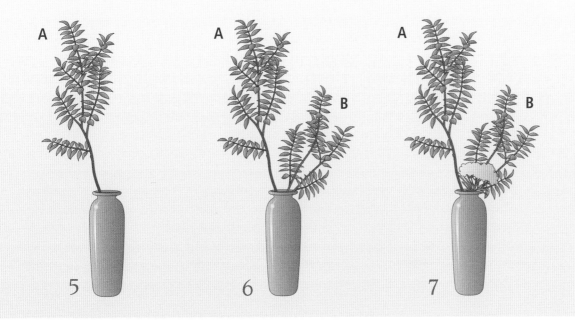

MAKING A TRUE CONNECTION WITH NATURE

The masters of Kado are keen observers of nature for they understand that nature is our greatest teacher. Whenever mankind ravages the Earth for her precious minerals or covers creation with concrete and buildings, nature always returns to restore the balance. Nature brings everything back into harmony and if you visit a disused quarry or a piece of derelict inner-city land, you will see nature slowly but surely returning things to their natural state. At first just a few small plants grow from seeds carried by the wind or dropped by passing birds. Later small trees appear and annually drop their foliage to help restore the soil and as the years go by, the imprint of man fades and the plants and animals reclaim what was originally theirs.

Nature also shows us how to be balanced. She grows warming vegetables for us to eat in the winter and cooling ones for the heat of summer. She shows by her example that the spring and summer are the best times for creativity and that autumn and winter are more suited to consolidation. In the summer season we plant and grow whereas in the winter season we harvest and store. All Zen practice is about discovering our true inner nature and part of this practice also involves discovering the true outer nature of creation. For when we are internally balanced, we are at one with the whole of creation.

We often take nature for granted and lose sight of her in our busy hectic lives. Do you know what phase the moon is at right now? How is nature responding to the season? What birds are more abundant, which plants are in bloom? A Kado Master knows the answers to all these questions and much more besides. Nature teaches him how things need to be if they are to be balanced and his arrangements are a sign of his understanding and interpretation of this balance. If you really want to experience Kado, just take a walk outside and open your senses.

Making a true connection with nature is achieved through the use of all five senses. Most people only look and perhaps listen to nature but when one uses all five senses to their full capacity, a huge panorama unfolds before us. Did you know that when the wind changes direction it smells different? Are you aware that a full moon feels different to a new moon? Have you noticed how the air tastes when there is incoming rain? These may sound like koans, for how can the wind have a smell, the moon a feel and the air a taste? Open your senses and you will discover that these things are real physical experiences; the wind really does have a smell and the air has a taste. Ask anyone who works everyday with children and they will tell you that children tend to be more excitable around the full moon. The children feel the moon and so do you although you are probably not aware of it.

Students of Zen strive for a true connection with nature because they understand that nature, like a student, is always seeking balance and harmony.

Whenever you are out in nature take a few moments to appreciate the magnificence and beauty of creation and understand that it mirrors your true self.

Next time you take a walk in the park or in the countryside, open all your senses to appreciate creation. Look at the beauty around you; see the way nature blends colour, line and form to create arrangements that are beautiful and pleasing to the eye. Listen to the wind in the trees and the song of the birds. Hear the sounds of insects and of running water. Smell the air and the plants, not just the sweet-smelling flowers but all the plants and trees. Did you know that each species of tree has its own unique aroma? Taste the air and edible plants and feel them. You will be amazed at how rich and diverse nature is. If you want to know nature, don't only go out on fine, sunny days, but also go out in the wind and the rain. Rainy days show nature in a completely different light. Dead sticks and stones come alive as they glisten in the wet and every tree performs a dance as the rain drips on to its leaves.

CHADO –
THE ART OF TEA

*'The tea ceremony requires years of training and practice...
yet the whole of this art, as to its detail, signifies no more
than the making and serving of a cup of tea. The supremely
important matter is that the act be performed in the
most perfect, most polite, most graceful, most charming
manner possible.'*

LAFCADIO HEARN

THE WAY OF TEA

The Japanese Tea Ceremony is the active performance of Chado (*Cha* means 'tea', *Do* means 'the way'). It takes place in a teahouse called a *chasitsu*, which is usually either a small structure separate from the house or a special room within the house. The emphasis on the construction and internal decor of the *chasitsu* is rustic simplicity but with care and refinement so as to offer the utmost hospitality to guests. Its dimensions are small, often less than 3 sq m (30 sq ft) and at one end is the *tokonoma* or alcove in which is displayed a hanging scroll and/or a Japanese flower arrangement. In the centre there may be a *ro* or small sunken fireplace for heating the teakettle, especially during the winter months.

In a *chaji* or full Japanese Tea Ceremony the guests arrive and wait in the tea garden until the host summons them. Once summoned they ritually wash their hands and mouths in a stone basin and proceed along the *roji*, 'dewy path' to the *chasitsu*. Guests remove their shoes, enter through a small, low door in an act suggestive of humility and proceed to the *tokonoma* to admire the scroll and/or decorations therein. The host then seats the guests in order of prestige and the ceremony begins. All this takes place with the minimum of conversation so that the guests may enjoy and appreciate the atmosphere and refined spectacle created by the simple decor, the sounds of the fire and water and the aroma of incense.

The *chaji* is not unlike a play containing a first and second act punctuated by an intermission. It commences with the *shoza*, 'first act', in which the host serves a light meal (*kaiseki*), followed by sake, Japanese rice wine. The host then prepares charcoal in the fireplace for the first time (*shozumi*) after which the guests retire to the garden for 'the intermission'. The *goza*, 'second act', begins with the host preparing *koicha* (thick tea) in a highly ritualistic

manner and serving it to the guests beginning with the guest of honour. Before the host makes the tea, each utensil is carefully and ritually cleaned in precise order and using prescribed motions. The utensils are then placed in a specific arrangement, the tea measured out and the exact required amount of hot water is added. The tea is gently whisked, again using prescribed movements and finally it is served. The host then prepares the charcoal for a second time (*gozumi*) and prepares a *usucha* (thin tea), again in a prescribed and ritualistic manner.

After all the guests have taken tea, the host cleans all the utensils and again lays them out in a precise manner. The guest of honour respectfully requests that the host allows the guests to inspect and admire the utensils and the host respectfully agrees. All the utensils are examined with the utmost care and reverence, not least because some, especially the *chawan* (tea bowl), may be irreplaceable antiques that have been passed down over several hundreds of years. The host then collects the utensils; host and guests silently acknowledge each other and the guests leave the teahouse. Finally the host bows at the door and the ceremony is complete.

Tea is an important crop in Japan and the best tea is considered to be grown in the fertile earth at the base of mountains such as Mount Fuji.

THE HISTORY OF CHADO

Ritual tea-drinking originated in China and was brought to Japan along with Buddhism. In the early 9th century, Lu Yu wrote the Chinese *Ch'a Ching* (*The Classic of Tea*) detailing the correct manner for cultivation and preparation of tea. Lu Yu was strongly influenced by Chan (Zen) Buddhism and Zen Buddhist monks in Japan took on many of his ideas. Originally monks drank tea as a means of averting tiredness during long sessions of meditation but later, in the 12th century, it became used in religious rituals in Zen monasteries to honour the first Zen patriarch Bodhidharma.

By the 13th century, samurai warriors had begun preparing and drinking tea in a ceremonial manner and during the 15th century it spread into the general populace of Japan. Friends would gather together in a quiet and isolated atmosphere to drink tea and discuss the merits of the arts of calligraphy, flower-arranging, poetry and the tea ceremony itself. By this time the foundations of the tea ceremony were laid, imbued with Zen wisdom and the sense of honour and respect. Tearooms were created especially for the ceremony and etiquettes were formalized for every aspect of tea-making from the decor of the room to the utensils used.

The most famous master of the tea ceremony was Sen Rikyu, an aesthete at the court of Toyotomi Hideyoshi, the 16-century Japanese military dictator. He codified the tea ceremony and his teachings led to the development of new forms of architecture in the design of tearooms and gardens and in the arts of poetry, calligraphy and flower-arranging. He created

a style of ceremony known as *wabi* that is characterized by simplicity, humility and naturalism using simple, unadorned utensils and a restrained, rustic architectural space. He also emphasized the value of imperfection and asymmetry as a celebration of uniqueness.

It was at this time that simple, lead-glazed earthenware called *raku ware* was invented in Kyoto expressly for use in the tea ceremony. Raku pots are moulded entirely by hand as opposed to being thrown on a wheel so that each pot is totally unique. They are glazed in natural and subdued colours such as dark brown, straw-coloured, green, light orange and cream. A new manner of firing was created in raku ware to encourage imperfection and asymmetry. Traditionally pottery was warmed and matured in a cold kiln before firing but this new type of glazed pottery was placed in a hot kiln for only an hour. It was then rapidly cooled at air temperature. This kind of process places extreme stress on the pot creating unique effects such as pockmarks and crackling in the glaze. Irregularities and imperfections in raku tea bowls are highly prized and are usually featured prominently as the 'front' of the bowl.

Sen Rikyu created the first tea school, which not only taught the principles of tea-making but also acted as a kind of finishing school for soldiers from the provinces. Sen Rikyu introduced the style of *wabi* (meaning roughly 'simplicity' and 'the absence of ornament'). Since then many different schools have emerged with the two main ones today being the Omotesenke and Urasenke. Currently the Urasenke School is the most popular but there are also many lesser-known schools still active in Japan today. Each school has its own rituals, types of utensils, seasonal variations in the method and preparation of tea and codes of etiquette. There are, however, common features to all schools of Chado. The host usually wears a kimono while guests wear either a kimono or subdued formal wear. Guests perform ritual washing of the hands and mouth from a small stone basin and always remove their shoes before entering the tearoom. All schools emphasize honour, calmness and respect. Zen Master Koun Yamada (1907–89) summed up the essence of Chado as follows: 'A cup of tea has no thoughts…it tastes the same to Buddhists as it does to Christians. There is not the slightest difference there.'

'If anyone wishes to enter the Way of Tea, he must be his own teacher.'

SEN RIKYU

Many Japanese tea bowls used in modern ceremonies are valuable antiques. This stoneware tea bowl dates from around the 16th or 17th century.

THE PRINCIPLES OF CHADO

Sen Rikyu (1522–91) is the most well-known historical figure in the development of Chado and he is still much revered today. He introduced the concept of *ichi-go ichi-e* (meaning 'one time, one meeting'), an understanding that each meeting is unique and can never be reproduced and so should be treasured.

Sen Rikyu set out four principles for Chado that are still followed to this day. They are:

- *Wa*: harmony
- *Kei*: respect
- *Sei*: purity
- *Jaku*: tranquillity.

Wa

Harmony is created both between the participants of Chado and the implements used. Ceremonies are carried out with little or no spoken words so there is no opportunity for differences of opinions to be aired or for egos to get in the way. The utensils are simple and rustic in construction so that they are pleasing to the eye and in keeping with the concepts of humility and restraint. The atmosphere of the tearoom is designed to promote peace and harmony, and to be pleasing to all the senses, with uncluttered decor, sweet smelling incense and simple flower arrangements.

Kei

Respect is shown not only for the participants but also the utensils used. Guests wash their hands and rinse their mouths out before entering the *cha-shitsu* as a symbolic gesture of cleansing. The host bows to each of the guests and the guests bow in return. Each utensil is carefully cleaned and handled as if it were the most precious object on Earth. Indeed many of the tea bowls used in such ceremonies are very old (up to 400 years) and have been passed down from one master to another.

Sei

Purity is not only implied through the ritual cleansing of participants and utensils, but is achieved through the intent of host and guests. The tea ceremony is a transformational practice designed to open the senses and mind to a full appreciation of the moment. All participants share the same goal and like all Zen practices, this goal can only be achieved through a clear mind and pure intent. Humility, serenity, self-restraint and simplicity all combine to make the ceremony a 'pure' experience.

Jaku

Tranquillity is achieved through both atmosphere and action. The *cha-shitsu* is calm and uncluttered, the actions of host and guests are slow and deliberate, and each article of the ceremony is treated with slow and caring respect. From the preparation of the room to the cleaning of the utensils and the preparing of the tea to its pouring, all is done mindfully with appreciation of the unique and mellow beauty of the ceremony.

The Japanese tea ceremony is the celebration of the uniqueness of every moment. No two ceremonies are the same because a moment can never be recreated.

'When tea is made with water drawn from the depths of the mind, whose bottom is beyond measure, then we really have what is called cha-no-yu (literally 'hot-water tea').'

TOYOTOMI HIDEYOSHI

CHADO EQUIPMENT

The range and diversity of equipment used in Chado could fill several volumes and even the simplest of ceremonies requires a wide range of supplies. Here are some of the basic utensils used in Chado.

Fukusa

Fukusa is a small, square cloth made of silk and used for the ritual cleaning of the tea-making utensils. They are usually of one colour, plain, with no pattern. Men and women use different colours, as do people of different skill levels and for different ceremonies and schools. Men usually use purple cloths and women usually use red.

Here we can see some of the utensils used in a traditional tea ceremony including the tea caddy with tea scoop and tea whisk to the right along with the ceremonial cleaning cloth.

Hishaku

A *hishaku* is a long bamboo ladle used for transferring water to and from the iron pot which heats it. A larger version is also used for the ritual cleansing of the guests prior to entering the teahouse.

Chawan

The tea bowl, which is arguably the most important piece of equipment and invariably the most valuable, is called *chawan*. Bowls come in a wide variety of shapes and sizes depending on the type of ceremony, the type of tea and the season.

Every part of Chado is performed with grace, respect and beauty. Here a woman ceremonially whisks tea during a traditional Japanese tea ceremony.

Natsume/Cha-ire

There are two styles of tea caddy used in different ceremonies. The *natsume* is short with a flat lid, round bottom and made of lacquered or untreated wood. The *cha-ire* is ceramic and is tall and thin, with an ivory lid.

Chasaku

A *chasaku* is a tea scoop made from a single piece of bamboo with a nodule in its centre used to scoop tea from the caddy into the tea bowl.

Chasen

A *chasen* is a tea whisk carved from a single piece of bamboo used to stir the tea in the tea bowl.

Caring for the Utensils

All the utensils are handled with the utmost care at all times. They are washed and stored individually and even broken utensils are either carefully repaired or reverently disposed of. For instance, broken whisks are never simply discarded. Once a year, usually around May, they are taken to the local temple and burned in a special ceremony called *chasen koyo*.

A SIMPLE TEA CEREMONY

You can perform a simple tea ceremony to honour a friend and experience the flavour of Chado. You don't have to have a special room or equipment but can improvise with the things you have. Tidy your tearoom, removing excess clutter and perhaps covering things like the television with a cloth. The room should be conducive to meditation and not bombard the senses. In the middle of the room place two cushions, a tray's-width apart, for you and your guest. Prepare the tray with all the things you need (listed below) again improvising with what you have if needs be.

Invite a friend around and explain to them that you would like to honour your friendship by performing a simple Japanese-style tea ceremony for them. Before they arrive make sure everything is in place and perhaps light some incense. When your guest arrives, ask them to remove their shoes and wait outside the room. Do one final check that all is pleasing to the senses, invite your guest into the room and seat them on one of the cushions. You are now ready to begin your ceremony.

In the Zen tradition, whenever any kind of ceremony is performed, it is the intent and simplicity of thought and deed that are at the forefront of practice.

Tea Ceremony

YOU WILL NEED
- A tray
- A tea bowl
- A bamboo whisk
- A small wooden scoop
- A silk cloth
- A linen cloth
- A tea container with Sencha green tea in it (available from health stores, delicatessens and some supermarkets)
- Boiling water
- A waste water jar

1 With your guest seated, bring the tray of tea-making utensils and place it on the floor in front of your guest. Kneel down opposite your guest and take a few calming breaths while focusing on the utensils.

2 Take your silk cloth and slowly purify the utensils by wiping them with it. Take great care and treat each utensil with equal respect, as if you were handling and cleaning a special piece of priceless jewellery. Carefully fold the silk cloth and tuck it into your belt.

3 Pour a little hot water into the tea bowl to cleanse it and rinse the tea whisk in it before pouring the water into the waste water jar. Take your linen cloth and wipe the tea bowl dry.

4 Scoop a large and small scoop of tea into the bowl and pour on boiling water. Gently stir the tea in a clockwise direction for a minute using the tea whisk in your left hand.

5 Turn the bowl so that the front of it faces your guest and offer them tea.

6 Once your guest has drunk their fill, take the tea bowl and rinse it out pouring the water and leaves into the waste water jar.

7 Dry the bowl using the linen cloth and replace it in its original position. Place the linen cloth on the tray and stand up. Pick up the waste water jar, turn counter-clockwise away from your guest and take it out of the room. Return and take out the tray in the same manner.

8 Return once more and exchange a bow with your guest to mark the end of the ceremony.

CHADO TEACHINGS IN EVERYDAY LIFE

For one who follows the Zen path, the Chado principles of harmony, respect, purity and tranquillity are not just reserved for the tea ceremony but are a part of everyday life. What makes a master of Chado is someone who embodies these principles in his or her daily life so that when it comes to the performance of a tea ceremony, these things flow naturally without a need for thought or intent. In order for this to happen, one has to practise these principles in all possible circumstances.

In order for one to outwardly show harmony, respect, purity and tranquillity, these qualities must first be nurtured internally. How can we make our daily lives more harmonious? Acceptance is the key. If you accept with pleasure whatever life brings you, not judging things as good or bad, but understanding that all experience has valuable lessons to teach, your life will flow more harmoniously. If one accepts everyone for who they are, there is no need to argue with others for aren't they entitled to think and say

whatever they like? If you want to be free, free to think and speak freely, you must allow everyone you meet the same freedom. This is also a significant part of paying respect.

One does not demand respect, but rather commands it. To gain respect from others and to show others respect, you must first respect yourself. The more respect you show to your body, mind and spirit, the more respect you will both show and command. Respect for the body means eating foods that make the body healthy and not working it so hard as to do it damage. Respect for the mind means giving your Self time to just be. Daily meditation plays an important role here. Respect for the spirit means being true to your Self and holding your inner integrity; this implies being flexible on the outside but firm on the inside.

Purity is a more elusive quality, especially when it comes to day-to-day living. So often our thoughts and actions are diluted by random emotions and daydreaming. Whenever you do anything, do it one hundred percent giving it your full focus. In this way both your intent and actions will be pure. If you find your mind wandering, stop what you are doing and take a few moments to collect your Self and refocus on pure thought. When sitting, just sit; when cleaning, just clean; when driving, just drive.

Tranquillity is about having such an inner calmness that it spreads to and shines from every cell of your body so that everyone can witness it. Tranquillity is calmness of body, mind and spirit. It is having true inner peace and can only be achieved if the first three principles are already there. When someone is tranquil, their every move is graceful and calm, their gesture, words and tone are all conducive to creating an atmosphere that is harmonious, respectful and pure. In that moment, the wonder of creation from the death of an ant to the birth of new galaxies is experienced. This oneness with nature cannot be felt outside tranquillity.

'Once having understood, one should read the teachings of the sages many times.'

DOGEN

One of the great challenges in Zen is bringing your practice into your daily life so that it becomes a part of who you are.

A FINAL WORD

Zen can be practised by anyone, at any age and in any situation. In this modern world, stress is without doubt the single biggest cause of ill-health and suffering. Modern physicians all agree that one of the key factors in the rise in the West of heart disease, cancer and other life-threatening illnesses is our way of life. Zen teaches us mastery of stress through the simple act of 'letting go' and in doing so it opens up a doorway to happiness, health and freedom. The only prerequisite to studying Zen is an enquiring mind and there are no barriers beyond the Self to stop you from practising its principles. Zen is open to everyone, young and old, sick and healthy, rich or poor. It can be practised at any time and in any place for the rest of your life. From the moment you rise in the morning to the moment you fall asleep at night, Zen teaches a practical way to navigate through our daily lives.

As we have seen, Zen has its roots in the East and the Eastern (oriental) mind is very different from that of the Western (occidental) mind. The occidental mind is scientific in its approach to life and carefully sifts, weighs, isolates and classifies information, whereas the oriental mind simply comprehends the moment. The biggest barrier we have to understanding Zen is our own thinking. We live in a reality of causality endlessly dividing and separating our experiences into good and bad, right and wrong or fair and unfair. Zen teaches us a way of living beyond these self-limiting classifications. It teaches us to embrace everything with pleasure, not judging a situation as either good or bad but seeking only to learn from it. In this way we can begin to understand how to make the best of every situation we find ourselves in and to rise above any adversity. We begin to enjoy life from moment to moment rather than living on a roller coaster of happiness and sadness.

To choose to follow a Zen path is to choose to get to know who you really are. It is the most exciting adventure you will ever embark on, filled with highs and lows, deep challenges and great enlightenments. There is no 'right' way to follow Zen, for mistakes and failures are regarded as of equal, if not greater importance than successes. Everyone walks the path

Zen provides us with a bridge between the material and natural worlds, showing how they can both speak the same language to us.

in their own way, but any who walks it long enough will ultimately find that the answers they seek lie in simple, persistent practice.

If Zen has captured your imagination, if it has opened your awareness to the possibility of a better quality of life, then you are already walking the Zen path. Zen is practised first and foremost in the mind. Just by being aware of the principles of Zen means that you have begun to experience 'Living Zen'. You are a spiritual being, whether you realize it or not. If you follow your heart and listen to your intuition, Zen will teach you how to live as a spiritual being.

If you feel drawn to practise one of the Zen arts mentioned in this book, you will begin to realize your true potential. There are many kinds of spiritual beings and the path of Zen provides opportunities for all. Study the Zen martial arts and learn how to be a spiritual warrior, to stand without fear and not give your power away to others. Study Kado and learn how to bring beauty into all situations. Learn Shodo and understand the power in words or follow Chado and unlock the power of sharing honour with those you meet. There is no limit to where Zen can take

When you look out at the wonder of creation, remember that it is merely a reflection of the wonder of who you really are.

you, but it is not only the destination that is important, but also the journey.

If you keep on your Zen path, eventually after many months or perhaps years, you will begin to practise *gyodo* ('the true Way'). It will take no effort of body or mind for you will have become one with Zen. Gyodo means more than merely practising a particular path, it means that your path pervades every area of your existence. You walk at one with the universe in all undertakings, whether sitting or lying down, talking or being silent, washing or going to the toilet. Every thought, every gesture and every word is in perfect harmony with the spirit of true Zen. You no longer need to tell people about Zen because they come and ask you first. 'What is it about you that makes you so calm?' 'Why do you never seem to get upset, even when terrible things happen?' 'How do you remain so happy?' You will truly walk your talk – you will have become a bodhisattva.

GLOSSARY

Aikido 'The Way of Harmony'. Zen martial art developed in Japan in the 1940s by Ueshiba Morihei.

Bodhisattva A living Buddha who chooses to dedicate himself to helping others find enlightenment.

Buddha 'The Awakened One'. The name given to Siddhartha Guatama, who lived around 500 BCE and founded Buddhism; the name given to an enlightened being.

Buddhanature The inherent potential within all sentient beings to become a Buddha.

Budo 'The Way of Combat'. The code and practice of Japanese martial arts.

Bushido 'The Way of the Warrior.' The path of the samurai.

Chado 'The Way of Tea'. The Japanese tea ceremony.

Chasitsu Teahouse where Chado is practised.

Dharma The teachings of Buddha; universal truth.

Do The Way or art; the path of truth.

Dojo Practice hall where one practises the Way; used for Zen meditation and the martial arts.

Dokusan Private interview between a Zen teacher and his student.

Enlightenment The realization of one's true spiritual nature and therefore the true nature of all existence; spiritual awakening.

Enso A dynamic representation of the circle of infinity showing the balance of yin and yang and the vibrant movement of creation.

Hara The lower abdomen; the centre of physical ki.

Judo 'The Soft Way'. Zen martial art developed by Kano Jigoro in the late 19th century.

Kado The Japanese art of flower-arranging, now more commonly known as 'Ikebana'.

Karma The law of cause and effect; the fundamental teaching of Buddhism that all our actions have consequences on our future actions.

Kendo 'The Way of the Sword'. Japanese fencing, based on the swordsmanship of the samurai.

Ki ('Chi'in Chinese) Life-force, energy, spirit.

Kin-hin Zazen while walking, practised between periods of sitting meditation (zazen).

Koan A Zen paradox designed to point to ultimate truth. A koan cannot be solved through logical thinking, but only through awakening our deep, spiritual nature.

Kyudo 'The Way of the Bow'. The Zen martial art of Japanese archery.

Mahayana Literally, the Greater Vehicle; form of Buddhism that seeks to realize enlightenment for the benefit of all beings.

Mu A negative prefix; nothing.

Rinzai Japanese Zen school found by Eisai in which koans are used in zazen training. Students practise zazen facing the centre of the room.

Roshi A Zen master or teacher.

Samsara The cycle of birth, life and death to which all unenlightened beings are bound.

Samurai A Japanese warrior; the upper class of Japanese feudal society.

Sesshin Days of intense zazen practice under the guidance of a Roshi.

Shin Mind or spirit, also translated as intent.

Shodo The Japanese art of calligraphy.

Soto Japanese Zen school founded by Dogen in which one practises zazen without a goal. Students practise zazen facing the wall.

Sutra The spoken or written teachings of Buddha.

Tai The physical body (as used in martial arts).

Teisho An exposition of Buddha's teachings given by a Roshi to Zen students.

Tokonoma Alcove in a chasitsu used to display a flower arrangement and/or a hanging scroll.

Wabi The esoteric philosophy of simplicity and absence of ornament introduced by Sen Rikyu.

Wasa Martial art techniques.

Zazen The practice of Zen through sitting meditation.

Zen Zen designates the process of objectless concentration and absorption.

SOURCES FOR QUOTATIONS

Acker, William R.B., *Kyudo – the Japanese Art of Archery*, Charles E. Tuttle Co., 1998.

Bancroft, Anne, *Zen – Direct Pointing to Reality*, Thames & Hudson, 1987.

Batchelor, Martine, *Walking on Lotus Flowers*, Thorsons, 1996.

Claremon, Neil, *Zen in Motion*, Inner Traditions International, 1992.

Cleary, Thomas, *The Blue Cliff Record*, Shambhala, 1992.

Cleary, Thomas, *Minding Mind*, Shambhala, 1995.

Cleary, Thomas, *The Pocket Zen Reader*, Shambhala 1999.

Dalai Lama, *The Little Book of Wisdom*, Rider Books 2000.

Davey, H.E., *Brush Meditation,* Stone Bridge Press, California, 1999.

Deshimaru, Taisen and Nancy Amphoux, *The Zen Way to the Martial Arts*, Rider Books, 1983.

Enomiya-Lassalle, Hugo M., *The Practice of Zen Meditation*, Thorsons, 1992.

Hanh, Thich Nhat, *Zen Keys: A Guide to Zen Practice*, Bantam Doubleday Dell, 1995.

Humphreys, Christmas, *Zen, A Way of Life (Teach Yourself series)*, Hodder & Stoughton, 1962.

Kapleau, Roshi, *The Three Pillars of Zen*, Anchor Books, 1980.

Lee, Man-Tu, *The Japanese Tea Ceremony Gift Set*, Element, 1999.

Leggett, Trevor, *A First Zen Reader*, Charles E. Tuttle Co., 1998.

Massey, Patricia, *The Essentials of Ikebana*, Weatherhill, 1978.

March-Penney, John, *Japanese Flower Arrangement*, Hamlyn, 1969.

Mifune, Kyuzo and Francoise White, *The Canon of Judo: Classic Teachings on Principles and Techniques*, Kodansha, 2004.

Nishijima, G., and J. Langdon, *How to Practise Zazen*, Windbell Publications Ltd, 1977.

Ozawa, Hiroshi, Tamiko Yamaguchi and Angela Turzynski, *Kendo: The Definitive Guide*, Kodansha,1997.

Putin, Vladimir, Vasily Shestakov and Alexander Levitzky, *Judo: History, Theory, Practice*, North Atlantic Books, 2004.

Reed, William, *Shodo: The Art of Coordinating Mind, Body and Brush*, Japan Publications Trading Co., 1990.

Sasamori, Junzo, and Gordon Warner, *This Is Kendo: The Art of Japanese Fencing*, Tuttle Publishing, 1989.

Soshitusu Sen, *Chado: The Japanese Way of Tea*, Weatherhill/Tankosha, 2003.

Stryk, Lucien and Takashi Ikemoto, *The Penguin Book of Zen Poetry*, Penguin Books, 1995.

Sunim, Kusan, Stephen Batchelor and Martine Fages, *The Way of Korean Zen*, Weatherhill, 1985.

Ueshiba, Morihei, and John Stevens, *The Art of Peace*, Shambhala, 1993.

Wienpahl, Paul, *The Matter of Zen: A Brief Account of Zazen*, Allen & Unwin, 1965.

Westbrook, Adele, and Oscar Ratti, *Aikido and the Dynamic Sphere: An Illustrated Introduction*, Tuttle Publishing, 2001.

Wood, Ernest, *Zen Dictionary*, Penguin Books, 1977.

Wray, William, *Sayings of the Buddha*, Arcturus Publishing Ltd, 2004.

Yamamoto, Tsunetomo, Justin Stone and Minoru Tanaka, *Bushido: The Way of the Samurai*, Square One Publishing, 2002.

Yampolsky, Philip B., *The Zen Master Hakuin*, Columbia University Press, 1985.

Yu, Lu K'uan, *Ch'an and Zen Teaching*, Rider Books, 1961.

INDEX

ACKNOWLEDGEMENTS

This book is dedicated to my daughter Lara.

I would like to thank my partner Debbie for her unfailing support and wise insight during the writing of this book and also my Tai Chi teacher Simon Suckling, for sharing his understanding and experience. Thanks must also go to Brenda Rosen for her guidance and encouragement and all at Godsfield and Hamlyn for making this project a reality.

Andy Baggott
www.andybaggott.com

The Publishers would like to thank the following organisations and individuals for their kind permission to reproduce the pictures in this book. Please contact us if any acknowledgements have inadvertently been omitted.

AKG, London/Jean-Louis Nou 10. Alamy 179 top; /Archivberlin Fotoagentur GmbH 161; /NTPL 130. Bridgeman Art Library/Archives Chaumet 153; /Paul Freeman 174; /Private Collection 127, 144. Corbis UK Ltd 61, 152; /Bruce Burkhardt 35; /Catherine Karnow 159; /China Photos/Reuters 132; /China Span, LLC 26; /David Martinez 111; /Dimitri Iundt 129; /Gilbert Iundt 134; /Horace Bristol 177; /Leonard de Selva 13; /Lindsay Hebberd 184; /Michael S. Yamashita 19; /Phil Schermeister 178; /Sakamoto Photo Research 27, 123. Digital Vision 77. Eye Ubiquitous 105; /Patricio Goycoolea 22, 25, 36, 99, 101, 103, 104, 107, 109, 181; /Hutchison 138, 141, 154; /Paul Seheult 81; /Stuart Wilson 17; /Tim Page 94. Fumi Wada/www.japaneseshodo.com Japanese calligraphy. Getty Images 18, 30–31, 32, 44, 59, 63, 64, 67, 68, 69, 70, 72–73, 82, 89, 90, 97, 98, 102, 112, 114, 136–137, 168, 173, 185. Natasha's Boutique 152. New Orleans Museum of Art 85. Octopus Publishing Group Ltd 162–164, 167; /Mark Winwood 23. Panos/Jean Leo Dugast 79; /Jeremy Horner 16; /Jim Holmes 192; /Stephan Boness 15. The Picture Desk/Art Archive/Oriental Art Museum Genoa/Dagli Orti 145. Plum Village Practice Centre 40, 116. Photodisc 169. Shambhala Publications/www.shambhala.com 46–55. Sogetsu Foundation 160 top; /Iemoto Akane Teshigahara 160 bottom. Werner Forman Archive 65, 147; /Basho Kenshokai 146; /Boston Museum of Fine Arts 124; /Private Collection 120–121; /V&A Museum 125. World Religions 41. www.JudoInfo.com/Neil Ohlenkamp 128. Chaun Zhi 28.

Executive Editor Brenda Rosen
Managing Editor Clare Churly
Executive Art Editor Sally Bond
Designer Martin Lovelock
Picture Researcher Vickie Walters
Production Controller Simone Nauerth